Praise for
The Power of a Focused Heart

I am over ninety years of age and have preached for sixty-eight years. I've read thousands of books. *The Power of a Focused Heart* is one of the best and most timely books I know. It's a self-help book for individuals who want to discover the true meaning and purpose of life. It's also a wonderful resource to use with a discovery group of kindred folk. If you mean business about discovering who you are and why you are here, I recommend that you read this book.

—Dr. Kermit Long
Founding Pastor, Friendship House
Phoenix, Arizona
Former General Secretary, Board of Evangelism
The United Methodist Church

In her succinct and powerful manner, Mary Lou Redding reveals the spiritual essence of the Beatitudes, using concrete terms we can apply easily to ourselves. Her insight into Jesus' teaching not only encourages individuals to reflect and examine themselves as Christian disciples but also motivates local congregations toward social action and community ministries. Redding challenges those who want to be transformed into dynamic servants of Christ, motivating them to take God's grace to hurting humanity.

—Rev. Jennifer Bryan
Minister of Outreach and Evangelism
Lenexa United Methodist Church
Lenexa, Kansas

The Power of a Focused Heart

8 Life Lessons from *the Beatitudes*

Mary Lou Redding

UPPER ROOM BOOKS®
NASHVILLE

Cover design: Left Coast Design, Portland, OR
Cover image: Mitch Tobias / Masterfile
Interior design: Lamar Creative
First printing: 2006

Library of Congress Cataloging-in-Publication Data
Redding, Mary Lou, 1950–
    The power of a focused heart : 8 life lessons from the Beatitudes / Mary Lou Redding.
        p. cm.
    Includes bibliographical references.
    ISBN 0-8358-9818-0
1. Beatitudes—Textbooks. 2. Christian life—Biblical teaching—Textbooks. I. Title.
    BT382.R375 2006
    241.5'3—dc22   2005025207

Printed in the United States of America

For Rosalie,
who blesses our family
by her loving ways

Contents

Introduction

Welcome to this study. Over the next eight weeks, as we move through this book, we will look at a passage from the fifth chapter of the Gospel of Matthew called the Beatitudes. These sayings form part of a longer passage—the Sermon on the Mount—and they focus on qualities Jesus valued and embodied.

Jesus directed the Beatitudes not to the crowds but to the inner circle, the small group of disciples who traveled with him day by day. Like most readers of this book, his hearers were already followers who wanted to learn how to live more faithfully. In Matthew's presentation of these sayings, Jesus withdraws with the disciples to a private place and then sits down to speak, conscious of his role as teacher and of his listeners as learners. Jesus proceeds to do what he so often does: he makes statements that turn the usual order of things on its ear.

HOW TO USE THIS BOOK

This eight-week study of the Beatitudes guides readers to examine one saying each week. Though designed primarily for use in small groups, *The Power of a Focused Heart* may also be used by individuals as a self-guided study.

A leader's guide for small-group meetings comprises the last chapter of the book. The weekly sessions are designed to last one hour, and leadership may rotate among group members. Participants read one chapter of the book each week before the group meeting. If you begin the week by reading the chapter, that content can frame your Bible reading and reflection in the following days. Chapters can be read in about fifteen minutes. (The first chapter is a bit longer than the others because it sets the stage for understanding the form of the Beatitudes.)

Each chapter includes suggestions for five days of daily Bible readings and accompanying reading/journaling questions, with space provided in the book to record your thoughts and reactions. If you keep a spiritual journal, you may want to write your reflections there. If you do that, bring the journal with you to the weekly meetings, since participants will be invited to summarize or comment on what they wrote in the daily reflections. No one else will see what you write, and in the group sessions you will say only what you wish to say. If you have never written in a journal about your spiritual journey and your insights, please consider this study an opportunity to experiment with this ancient Christian practice. You may find, as I have, that writing in a journal helps you to attend more closely to God's work in your life. Sessions 5 and 6 call for additional materials available at no charge on the Internet; read the beginning of the Leader's Guide to find out more about this.

SETTING THE BEATITUDES IN CONTEXT

Matthew's Gospel is neatly organized. Beginning with a genealogy that shows how Jesus comes from the lineage of David, its stories are arranged chronologically through Jesus' life. The Gospel closes with the account of Jesus' final words to his disciples after the Resurrection.

The opening genealogy is followed by the stories of the Magi, Jesus' temptation, and the calling of the disciples at the beginning of Jesus' public ministry. Then Matthew presents Jesus' teachings on a variety of topics in the section known as the Sermon on the Mount, where the Beatitudes are found. This is followed by stories of Jesus' encounters with people and his miracles, interspersed with parables and, often, private explanations of them to the inner circle of the disciples. Near the end of the Gospel (chapters 23–25), just before the account of Jesus' arrest and crucifixion, Matthew includes another long discourse, this one about "final things"—the Judgment—including a series of parables about the nature of the kingdom of God. My greatly simplified outline of the Gospel of Matthew is meant to show a sort of "bookend" effect. The Gospel begins in the community of God's people, showing how Jesus fulfills the prophecies given in Hebrew scripture, and ends with Jesus' teaching about God's new community. The last section gives us his final promise to continue to support that community: "Remember, I am with you always, to the end of the age."

The Gospel of Matthew focuses on this transformed community that Jesus came to initiate. Matthew most frequently refers to the new community as the "kingdom of God" or the "kingdom of heaven," using both expressions interchangeably. Often he shortens the references to simply "the kingdom," as in "the good news of the kingdom" (24:14) or "children of the kingdom" (13:38). *Kingdom* and *king* are used more than seventy times in a theological sense in Matthew's twenty-eight chapters. Jesus tells us in Matthew 6:33 to make seeking the kingdom of God our first priority. The first beatitude (and also the last—another set of bookends) uses that phrase.

The Beatitudes take their title from the Latin word that begins each of them, a word translated as "blessed." Other English words derive from this same root—*beatific* and *beatify*, for instance. These related words all signal God's presence shining into the world through a human. In these sayings, Jesus identifies the qualities that allow this blessedness to happen. These qualities are the essence of what it means to live in the new kingdom where God's will is being done. Poverty of spirit, meekness, mourning, hungering for God's way, and all the other blessed states Jesus describes are not simply goals for behavior. They represent the outgrowth of the new heart God promises us. We will come closer to understanding their deep meaning if we remember that they are about community, about what happens within us and through us as we live in the presence of God with other believers.

Over the next few weeks, you will have the opportunity to hear Jesus' words again, explore their meanings, and discover your response. I think you will also discover that the Beatitudes are not easy sayings we can glibly incorporate into our way of life. Like so much of what Jesus said, they invite us to move beyond our first impressions and surface meanings. They challenge us to explore. Your fellow travelers will be a resource to you, as you will be to them, over the coming weeks. Your honest questions and prayerful reflection will become part of the bread for the journey. Welcome to the expedition!

BLESSED ARE YOU

When Jesus saw the crowds, he went up the mountain; and after he sat down, his disciples came to him. Then he began to speak, and taught them, saying:

"Blessed are the poor in spirit, for theirs is the kingdom of heaven.

"Blessed are those who mourn, for they will be comforted.

"Blessed are the meek, for they will inherit the earth.

"Blessed are those who hunger and thirst for righteousness, for they will be filled.

"Blessed are the merciful, for they will receive mercy.

"Blessed are the pure in heart, for they will see God.

"Blessed are the peacemakers, for they will be called children of God.

"Blessed are those who are persecuted for righteousness' sake, for theirs is the kingdom of heaven.

"Blessed are you when people revile you and persecute you and utter all kinds of evil against you falsely on my account. Rejoice and be glad, for your reward is great in heaven, for in the same way they persecuted the prophets who were before you."

—MATTHEW 5:1-12

Then [Jesus] looked up at his disciples and said:
"Blessed are you who are poor,
      for yours is the kingdom of God.
"Blessed are you who are hungry now,
      for you will be filled.
"Blessed are you who weep now,
      for you will laugh.
"Blessed are you when people hate you, and when they exclude you, revile you, and defame you on account of the Son of Man. Rejoice in that day and leap for joy, for surely your reward is great in heaven; for that is what their ancestors did to the prophets.
"But woe to you who are rich,
      for you have received your consolation.
"Woe to you who are full now,
      for you will be hungry.
"Woe to you who are laughing now,
      for you will mourn and weep.
"Woe to you when all speak well of you,
      for that is what their ancestors did to the false prophets."

—LUKE 6:20-26

The Blessings of Poverty

Blessed are the poor in spirit,
for theirs is the kingdom of heaven.

—MATTHEW 5:3

Have you ever been truly in need? Have you been hungry with no money to buy food? Did you work your way through college, so poor you couldn't buy the books you needed and using borrowed ones to study? Did you struggle as a young parent to pay for childcare? Did your car break down when you needed it to get to work but had no money to pay for repairs? Take a moment to recall the feelings you had at some time when you were in need and had no resources to get what you needed. Would you describe yourself in that situation as feeling blessed? What does being in need feel like? While holding that idea in your mind, hear Jesus saying, "Blessed are the poor in spirit." Can you reconcile being poor with being simultaneously "blessed"? Yet that is what Jesus says in this first beatitude.

That word, *blessed,* begins each of the Beatitudes. Though Jesus' hearers were familiar with this word, it is not one we use often in everyday speech. The Greek word translated "blessed" is *makarios.* It means "fortunate," "well-off," or "happy" and is the same word Mary used in the Magnificat when she said, "All generations will call me blessed" (Luke 1:48). But the word is not simply an adjective. Wisdom literature and prophecies often use statements of blessing in the form of the Beatitudes, as in "Blessed are all those who wait for [the LORD]" (Isa. 30:18). These statements, called *makarisms,* come from the root word *makarios.* Such statements are more than just an opinion. Their sense and impact may be clearer if we look at another makarism that appears in Jeremiah 17:5-8:

> Thus says the LORD:
> Cursed are those who trust in mere mortals
>   and make mere flesh their strength,
>   whose hearts turn away from the LORD.
> They shall be like a shrub in the desert,
>   and shall not see when relief comes.
> They shall live in the parched places of the wilderness,
>   in an uninhabited salt land.
>
> Blessed are those who trust in the LORD,
>   whose trust is the LORD.
> They shall be like a tree planted by water,
>   sending out its roots by the stream.
> It shall not fear when heat comes,
>   and its leaves shall stay green;
> in the year of drought it is not anxious,
>   and it does not cease to bear fruit.

In this passage we see what Jesus' hearers already knew: the form commonly consists of two parts, a positive statement that begins "Blessed . . ." and a negative statement that begins "Cursed . . ." and states the opposite behavior or attitude. Such two-part structures occur often in Hebrew wisdom literature—Job, Psalms, Proverbs, and Ecclesiastes. Proverbs 10 contains a succession of these—thirty-two balanced sayings, each a positive statement followed by a negative (or the reverse). For example, "A wise child makes a glad father, but a foolish child is a mother's grief," and, "The LORD does not let the righteous go hungry, but he thwarts the craving of the wicked" (Prov. 10:1, 3). Jesus' hearers would have recognized that the form implied a comparison. They might, in fact, have automatically supplied the opposites of each of the Beatitudes as they considered their meanings.

Looking more closely at a passage from Isaiah 30 gives us a clue to the source of the power in heeding these words. Verse 18 says, "Therefore the LORD waits to be gracious to you; therefore he will rise up to show mercy to you. For the LORD is a God of justice; blessed are all those who wait for him." Isaiah's statement is true and powerful not simply because Isaiah says it but because it is rooted in a truth about the nature of God. Our gracious God longs to show compassion and reach out to us. Even when we run away, as the people Isaiah addressed were running, God still longs to be gracious to us. Anyone who waits on and trusts this God is indeed blessed.

Even more, one who trusts in this God can be assured that because of God's power and nature, what God's messenger promises will come to pass. God's gracious purpose will not be thwarted; justice will come. Such statements of blessing are rooted in truths about God and God's ways, about what God wants for us. Psalm 1 (which echoes Jeremiah 17:7-8, referred to previously) begins with "Blessed is the [one] who does not walk in the counsel of the wicked . . ." and ends by saying why: "For the LORD watches over the way of the righteous" (NIV). In other words, when we attempt to live as God wants, we already walk the way of blessedness—because God's power moves with us and carries us along. These "Blessed . . ." statements declare what God wants for all believers—in our actions and on God's side in response.

But if this is the case, why don't the Beatitudes stipulate that God will respond, as the passage in Isaiah does? Again, Jesus' hearers would have known the reason. The absence of mention of God indicates reverence for God. One of the Ten Commandments tells us not to take God's name in vain. In common practice, devout Jews extend this commandment into reluctance to speak God's name at all. They consider God's name so holy that unclean human lips should never utter it. So in talking about God, devout Jews may use what is called the "divine passive" construction, not naming an actor but with the common understanding that the unnamed actor is God. In sayings like the Beatitudes, the speaker and the hearers understood that God gives the kingdom ("theirs is the kingdom"), God would comfort ("they will be comforted"), God would show mercy ("they will receive mercy"), and so on. When they listened to the Beatitudes, Jesus' hearers knew that he was talking about what God would do, because they understood he used the form that avoids speaking God's name.

And so in the saying "Blessed are the poor in spirit, for theirs is the kingdom of heaven," Jesus' audience would probably have been stopped not by the form but by his saying poverty was a blessed state. Those who listened to Jesus that day did not consider being poor a blessing. In fact, the poor were at a perpetual disadvantage because they were unable to observe "the minute regulations of purity"[1] that strict Jews observed. Poor people could not keep the dual kitchens required by kosher dietary laws. They could not afford two sets of utensils, two sets of pans to cook in, two sets of dishes to eat from. They did not have indoor plumbing or servants and therefore could not avoid the contact with bodily fluids that would make them ritually unclean. In their daily work they could not avoid other "unclean" people. These realities made them perpetually unacceptable and unwelcome in the Temple and relegated them to a lower place in the hierarchy of Judaism.

So for those who wanted to live as the Law directed, poverty represented an obstacle to holiness, not a blessing. We think of the stories of Jesus feeding crowds of thousands as heartwarming miracles, but to strict Jews these meals would have been scandalous.[2] Good Jews did not eat with unwashed, ritually impure people. Jesus flew in the face of their conventions when he mingled with such people and encouraged clean and unclean to eat together. When Jesus said that the kingdom of God belongs to the "poor" (Luke 6:20) or "the poor in spirit" (Matthew's version), he overturned the usual way of thinking about who has the inside track with God.

WHAT IS POVERTY?

What does it mean to be poor? Being poor means lacking the coin of the realm—whatever "realm" we're operating in. In athletics, the coin of the realm is coordination, speed, agility, competitive spirit. In academics, it is ability to memorize, to recall facts, to write, to take tests well. In our culture obsessed with physical appearance, the coin of the realm is a perfect nose, flat abs, white teeth, flawless skin—or having sufficient coin to get them via the local plastic surgeon. In the spiritual life, we may think of the coin of the realm as knowledge of the Bible, the ability to pray or to adhere to a particular pattern of prayer, unflagging willingness to obey God, the desire to read about spiritual matters. But this is not the model or standard Jesus talks about in this beatitude. Jesus says that the kingdom of God belongs to those who have little or nothing spiritually. Have you ever felt spiritually inadequate? Have you said, "God, there's no way I can do this"? Then, Jesus says, you're the kind of person who will fit right into this new community God is building! In fact, you and people like you will be running things! The entire kingdom will belong to you.

Jesus was drawing a picture of a different kind of spiritual life. He told his followers, "Unless your righteousness exceeds that of the scribes and Pharisees, you will never enter the kingdom of heaven" (Matt. 5:20). The Pharisees prided themselves on keeping literally hundreds of religious rules. How could anyone exceed that? In this beatitude, Jesus said in effect, intimacy with God means moving beyond rules. In Matthew 5:20 and here in the Beatitudes, Jesus was saying what he said often, in many settings: the spiritual life is not about rules; true spirituality is about relationship. It is not about how well we pray or how many Bible verses we can quote. It is about living in relationship with God, depending upon God daily.

This beatitude offers us a spiritual life based not on performance but on dependence. For people like us, such a concept is tough to grasp and even tougher to embrace. We have been socialized in a culture where rugged individualism and self-determination permeate our way of thinking. In fact, most of us would probably prefer to talk about putting our money where our mouth is or about faith without works being dead. An individualistic approach keeps us in control, makes us feel as if we are in charge of our spiritual lives. We can't conceive of what it would mean to *desire* poverty of spirit, to depend on God for everything.

A friend of mine told me about a woman who caused her to think in new ways about what it means to depend absolutely on God. My friend and her husband were living in Panama, where he served with the U.S. military. Like most families there, they had a household servant, a woman I will call Mrs. Green. About seventy years old, Mrs. Green had worked as a maid all her life. Her country had no social security, no government retirement program. She had always lived day to day, never earning enough to be able to save, and she was a widow without family to help support her. But she spoke continually and joyously of God's goodness and faithfulness in supplying her needs—as God was doing through providing the job in my friend's home. She also acknowledged that she was getting on in years and would not be able to work indefinitely. My friend asked her one day, "What will you do when you can no longer work? Where will you live?"

"Well, honey," Mrs. Green replied with peaceful evenness, "I'll just go and live under the bridge with all the others like me. The Lord will keep on taking care of me, just as he always has!" Mrs. Green meant literally the remark about living under the bridge. She portrayed poverty of spirit, joyfully acknowledging that the same God who had given her jobs and the daily strength to perform them would continue caring for her when she could no longer work, even if she had to live under a bridge. Because she already realized that God supplied all her needs, a change in circumstances would mean little.

God is the one who, as Deuteronomy 8:18 says, gives us "power to get wealth." Anything we possess is ours because God has graciously allowed us to have it. This flies in the face of our culture's prattling about personal power and self-development, where we make ourselves into what we want to be. People like Mrs. Green remind us that none of us can claim to be self-made; every good gift in our lives comes from God's grace flowing toward us.

PARTNERSHIP WITH GOD

Even the raw materials we use are God's gifts. Our talents, intelligence, energy, skill—all the raw materials of our "self-made" successes—are themselves gifts. We owe everything we are to God's grace and generosity. Someone recently sent me a funny story that emphasizes this truth—and our blindness to it. In the story, someone comes to God with various complaints about humans, claiming he could make a better, more efficient model. God agrees to a person-building contest, and the two prepare to begin. But as the challenger reaches for a handful of earth, God says, "Oh, no—you have to provide your own dirt." That image shows how limited we are, how little we have apart from God's provision, and how blind we are to that fact.

When we recognize and acknowledge our absolute inability to meet even our smallest needs without God's help, we begin to move toward being "poor in spirit." In the aftermath of Hurricane Katrina, like many Americans, I watched hours of television coverage. Time after time, evacuees spoke of having escaped the storm with nothing more than the clothes they wore. I tried to imagine what it would feel like to be in their situation, to own nothing more than the blue jeans and old shirt I am wearing as I write these words. I would feel vulnerable, I'm sure, having to depend completely on others for food, shelter, and the resources to build a future. Perhaps thinking of ourselves as this utterly dependent on God could help us understand what Jesus meant in this beatitude.

Poverty of spirit involves realizing that we cannot do what God wants by depending on our own skills, insight, or energy. This realization becomes the gate into God's kingdom. If you've ever felt overwhelmed, aware of how impossible it is for you to do what God asks, you've been in touch with what it means to be "poor in spirit." In this beatitude Christ invites us into a partnership that can change us and, through us, change the world: "All of you who know you can't possibly do it, you're the ones I want. You're just the kind of people I can use."

Realizing our poverty of spirit means an end to business as usual. The recovery movement has a saying, "If you keep doing what you've always done, you'll keep getting the results you've always gotten." Jesus was not reinforcing the status quo. He invited his followers to change their way of thinking about themselves and about what God asked of them. He opened the door to a new way. Johannes Metz says in his wonderful book *Poverty of Spirit* that owning our spiritual poverty is the beginning of becoming fully human, what God intends us to be, because it frees us to put aside our own ideas about what we want to do and be.

As we acknowledge that the spiritual life depends totally on God's working in and through us, we are freed to develop in our individual, unique ways as we follow God. Some of the hurricane evacuees I mentioned earlier seemed to glimpse the opportunity in their situations. They spoke having having the slate wiped clean, of looking forward to building a new life. Being stripped of what they had trusted opened a door to think about their lives in a new way. Perhaps acknowledging our poverty in spiritual matters could help us allow God to reshape us and direct us to live differently. Perhaps we could let go of others' ideas and expectations and allow ourselves to be what God calls us to be.

Only God can guide us into the full meaning of our poverty. "The individual guises of this poverty are the possibilities bestowed on us by God. . . . They are the chalice that God holds out to us," says Metz.[3] None of us can drink this chalice to the last drop, for none of us can be perfectly obedient. Partial obedience and partial knowledge of God are all that any of us is capable of—which brings us again to our poverty of spirit. In fact, acknowledging it is an act of faith. We don't need faith at the points where we feel capable personally and sure theologically. We need faith when we feel inadequate and unsure; those are the times most of us become most aware of our need for God.

Those who know how much they need God can live into reality the new way that Jesus envisioned. The "poor in spirit" are the ones God names as the heirs of the kingdom. As we live this beatitude, Christ's new kingdom becomes visible in us.

Can we yearn to be like Mrs. Green? Can we surrender the heavy mantle of trying to be, as someone has described us in our drivenness, "General Manager of the Universe"? Many of us are so accustomed to trying to be good—doing what is right, covering everything on our to-do list—that we live our lives, even our spiritual lives, at a frantic pace. We cram every minute of every day with activity and achievement, measuring our worth by what we earn or what good deeds we have done. But this beatitude says that approach is all wrong. When we offer to God what we cannot be or do—our weaknesses—then the kingdom is ours. God says in this beatitude, "When you give up your illusions of control and power and acknowledge your absolute need for me, all that I have opens to you."

With God, those who realize their poverty have everything.

DAILY REFLECTIONS: CHAPTER 1

Day 1—Read 1 Kings 17:1-16.

God fed Elijah by sending ravens. Think back on a time of extremity in your life. How did God "feed" you? How did God sustain you when the situation seemed almost hopeless?

According to this passage, God performed miracles day after day to feed the widow, her son, and Elijah. Do you think God still miraculously meets people's needs? If so, why? If not, why not?

In what areas of your life do you feel inadequate or overwhelmed? Where are you aware that you truly need God because you can't handle a situation on your own?

Day 2—Read Isaiah 10:12-13 and 17-20.

What phrases from the king of Assyria's speech convey arrogance? Have you heard people say similar things?

Are there times when it is right to take pride in our accomplishments? Where do you draw the line between arrogance and an honest sense of accomplishment when you have worked hard?

What do you think it means to "lean on the Lord . . . in truth," as verse 20 says God's people will do?

Day 3—Read Deuteronomy 8:11-18.

This passage seems to say that prosperity presents a special problem or temptation to people of faith. What challenges come with wealth? Does prosperity work against living with a sense of poverty of spirit?

How much of the credit for what we have is ours, and how much is God's?

What cultural attitudes or beliefs make it difficult to depend on God? Do you think depending on God is easier for people in less affluent settings than it is for us?

Day 4—Read Matthew 15:21-28.

How does the woman in this passage reflect poverty of spirit?

Those who looked down on this woman judged her unworthy, but she persisted in asking Jesus for what she needed. What does her persistence say to you about poverty of spirit?

How can we balance efforts to get what we need with dependence on God?

Day 5—Read John 15:1-8.

What are some things we can do to "abide" in the Vine, to stay connected to Christ and grow spiritually?

How do you feel when you read Jesus' words, "Apart from me you can do nothing" (v. 5)? In what areas of life do you need Christ's help right now?

Rewriting This Week's Beatitude

As the reading for this week outlines on page 16, Jesus and his hearers were familiar with the form "Blessed are . . . Cursed are . . ." or "Blessed are . . . Woe to . . ." His hearers knew that the positive statements had negative opposites; they might have supplied these almost without thinking. Write your understanding of this week's beatitude and a "Cursed are . . ." or "Woe to . . ." opposite statement:

Positive: _____ are those who

_____

_____.

Negative:

_____

_____.

Notes for Group Session

My response to this week's beatitude will be

_____

_____.

The Gifts in Our Grieving

**Blessed are those who mourn,
for they will be comforted.**

—MATTHEW 5:4

Some time ago I called the home of a friend who had died a few weeks earlier to speak to one of her sons before he returned to college. But he wasn't there, and the answering machine picked up. The recorded message on the machine hadn't been changed, and I was unprepared for the stab of sadness I felt on hearing the distinctively husky voice of his mother, "Hi. This is Karen. . . ." For the rest of that day, sadness welled up strongly in me from time to time, unpredictably and unbidden. At one point I found myself walking down the hall at work, brushing tears from my cheek as I realized again that she really is gone from our lives, especially from her children's lives. I did not feel "blessed." At the least, such sadness is an inconvenience in the midst of all the other tasks we are doing and need to do; at its heaviest, the weight of deep mourning can immobilize us. Yet Jesus said, "Blessed are those who mourn." This statement runs contrary to common sense. Someone who mourns has suffered a loss and is grieving. To be in that situation is not a blessing. What could Jesus have meant? How could mourning ever be a blessing?

OUR RELUCTANCE TO MOURN

Most of us are reluctant to mourn. In some cultures, mourning is formalized, with specific practices and costume expected. Even our culture expected this in past generations. In the novel *Gone with the Wind*, Scarlett O'Hara scandalizes a gathering by dancing with Rhett Butler before her formal year of mourning for her husband is over, while she is still wearing the widow's black garb. These ideas are not found only in novels. As recently as the early 1900s, widows were expected to wear black for a season of mourning after the death of their husbands. In Jesus' time, professional mourners often were hired to wail outside the home of a family whose loved one had died. (Jeremiah 9:17 mentions these people, and in the story of the healing of Jairus's daughter [Matt. 5:23; Mark 5:38; Luke 8:52], Jesus and Jairus arrive to find the mourners already present.)

But mourning is not as public these days as it once was. Many of us feel ill at ease around those who are sad about the death of someone they love. Some even believe that Christians should not grieve openly or deeply, that to do so signifies lack of faith. John Wesley once wrote a letter to one of the clergy in his charge accusing the man of "inordinate affection" for grieving the death of his beloved daughter. Though most of us would never say that sort of thing to a grieving parent, I have heard people comment on a mourner's composure as a sign of strong faith. Such comments imply that tears, distress, and other shows of strong emotion signal that the mourner is somehow not depending on or trusting God.

Many of us are not eager to experience mourning even vicariously, much less firsthand by acknowledging our own losses and sadness. It is as if we want to build a wall around our heart to contain the pain and keep it far from us because we fear that we could be swept away by the power of our own feelings. Sometimes denying our hurt seems easier than facing life's wounds and grieving for what we have lost or for what we realize we cannot have.

That makes sense, in a way. Who wants to experience pain? Addictions are often described as people's attempts to numb themselves, to dull inward pain by using drugs or drinking or working compulsively—anything to avoid the mourning that comes with acknowledging our inward hurt. For that's what mourning is. The second half of this beatitude tells us why we can experience blessing when we mourn: in the terrifying solitude of our pain, we can meet God. Note that this beatitude does not say that all suffering will be resolved, that those who mourn will be delivered, that their problems will be resolved, or that what they lost will be restored. Mourning offers a deeper and better result—our losses and pain can connect us with God. This is good news for us because, in human terms, when we mourn we are always alone.

THE SOLITUDE OF MOURNING

Even when in a group mourning one person's death, each of us mourns a unique loss. When someone I care about dies, what I lose is different than what other friends of that person lose. No one can ever be that person to me again. No one else can know the laughter I have shared with that friend, the confidences we entrusted to each other, the words we exchanged in quiet times together. Other mourners can know what they will miss and the depth of their pain, but they cannot know exactly what I feel. Only God can know what I mourn.

Something similar is true of us in the lesser, small deaths and losses that life brings. Consider the death of an opportunity or of a dream. No one can know what happens within us as we nurture particular dreams. No one can know how many nights we lay awake, smiling in the dark as we contemplated the vision of our realized dream. No one can know how many choices in our lives were shaped by that dream, how many sacrifices we made for it, how that dream affected our choices and moved us along. No one can know the importance of my dreams to the whole structure and appearance of who I am. So when I must acknowledge that the dream will never come to fruition, no one else can know my grief precisely. No one can know the pain within us when we think about lost innocence, lost opportunities, lost years before we came to awareness of God. In that sense each of us always mourns alone—except that this beatitude promises us God is there. "Will be comforted" reminds us that God comes to those who mourn and longs to embrace them.

The book of Job offers us a clear picture of someone who discovers the power of this encounter. Job loses his possessions, his children, his health. Eventually, even his comforters turn on him, accusing him of bringing his suffering on himself. At one point Job sits in ashes, using a shard of pottery to scrape the boils that cover his body. His children and his wealth are gone. He cries out, wrestling with God and questioning. Yet this does not weaken his relationship with God. God does not turn away. In the final chapter of the drama, Job affirms a new intimacy and reality in his faith, saying to God, "I had heard of you by the hearing of the ear, but now my eye sees you." This is one of the gifts of mourning: in the terrifying solitude of our tears, we can see God and come to know God at a new depth, because God embraces us and sustains us as we weep. When we accept pain and loss as inevitable parts of life, we find that God shares them with us. And that realization changes us as well as the pain. It can also change the way we see life.

THE GIFT OF SEEING

I have witnessed such a change in a coworker I used to consider annoyingly cheerful. You've probably known someone like him—always exuberant, even at ridiculously early hours. I'd meet him in the parking lot, muttering and groaning as I typically do in the early morning, only to be greeted with his huge smile. He always had something positive to say, and he said it with energy and enthusiasm, responding to my "realism" with little jokes and words of faith in God. Even his memos about dry and boring official business were cheerful and funny. Honestly, I could not understand how anyone could be so unremittingly upbeat. Then he became seriously ill. The memo notifying us of his absence from the office also mentioned that this was a recurrence of cancer from several years earlier, and in a flash I understood his joy in living and his open-armed embrace of life. I had seen it before in others, and I know it comes from having been close to death. He appreciates the small gifts of each day with a depth and consistency that judge me in my grousing and complaining. From that moment he became my favorite picture of another gift that can be found in our mourning, in our tears: the gift of entering into life fully and learning to savor it.

A saying attributed to poet Edwin Markham goes like this: "Sorrows come to stretch out spaces in the heart for joy." Often those who seem to most enjoy life have endured great loss or pain. Some years ago a man named Orville Kelly was diagnosed with terminal cancer and told he had only a short time to live. Devastated by the diagnosis, Mr. Kelly for a while was overwhelmed by grief at the prospect of losing his life and leaving his family. But then he determined that if he had only a short time to live, he would live each day to the fullest. His personal mission to live life fully day by day became a nationwide campaign, and he wrote a book and founded an organization called Make Today Count. The organization helps people learn to see and enjoy the good in every day. Defying death by affirming life, for the next twenty-plus years Mr. Kelly spread the message that each day brings wonderful gifts and opportunities for those whose eyes remain open to them. Like my coworker, in facing his grief and mortality, Orville Kelly came to embrace life more fully and taught others to do the same.

THE GIFT OF FEELING

Allowing ourselves to mourn develops our capacity to feel life's joys. I believe that positive and negative emotions are two sides of the same coin. Of course, many of us would prefer to experience and deal with only positive feelings. We often feel uncomfortable with our own or others' sadness, anger, disappointments, fears. I once was in a relationship with a man who loved my intensity about the things I like. When I enjoy something, I really throw myself into it. However, when I am sad or angry, I really throw myself into those emotions as well. This man wanted me to express my positive emotions and bury the ones he saw as negative. He didn't think Christians ought to get angry or sad; he said it was "a bad witness." I see things differently. Our emotions are bundled together, interconnected. If we push down our sadness and never face it, we inevitably close off other emotions as well—and that limits our experiencing life. Yes, being human brings hurts—but it also offers many delights. As we learn to feel all of our feelings, we explore what it means to be fully human, to be all that God created us to be.

Mourning is one way we acknowledge life as a precious gift. In fact, acknowledging our vulnerability and fragility can engender a posture of gratitude, for when we realize how fragile our existence is, we both hold on more lightly to the gifts life brings and appreciate them more deeply.

A friend of mine told a story about her mother's burial that helps me remember how important a statement our mourning can be. After the interment, my friend found herself saying, "They stopped traffic for you today, Mom. All those people we passed on the way to the cemetery— they stopped their cars and honored you. They said that your life mattered." When we mourn, we say that the person or dream or relationship we mourn, mattered. Each person's life counts for something, and anyone's death is a loss. As simple an act as pulling aside to let a funeral procession pass affirms the basic goodness of life and the worth of the one who died.

THE GIFT OF COMPASSION

Appreciating life's goodness does not mean we become Pollyannas who deny life's difficult realities and opt for superficial platitudes. In our mourning, as we allow God to comfort us, we come to see that others mourn too. The God who weeps with and for us longs for fullness of life for each one of us. As we allow ourselves to mourn our own losses, we discover the depth of the world's pain. The prophet Jeremiah said, "For the hurt of my poor people I am hurt, I mourn. . . . Is there no balm in Gilead?" (Jer. 8:21-22). God longs for wholeness and joy for each of us and for all of creation. When we allow ourselves to be drawn close to God by our own hurts and losses, we will discover the compassion of God's tender heart. And if we allow ourselves to be shaped by God, we will find our hearts drawn to others who hurt.

This is part of the challenge for us in this second beatitude. But as I said earlier, we humans want to draw back from what is painful. And so we face a choice: Will we allow ourselves to mourn our own losses and to mourn with God for the pains of our broken world? Or will we insulate ourselves from them? It is possible to live our lives within narrowly prescribed boundaries, to stay within what is safe, familiar, and undemanding. We can refuse to respond to the real and sometimes carefully hidden pain of those in our churches and neighborhoods. We can close our eyes to the needs of our towns; to the hungry and the lonely; to those without adequate housing, jobs, and health care. We can close our eyes to the world beyond our towns, to the drug culture that corrupts many inner-city neighborhoods, to the civil wars and famines that have stolen the childhood of an entire generation in some African countries. We can refuse to be touched by the plight of the discarded children of Brazil or of eastern Europe. It is easy to see why we might be tempted to do so. "Compassion fatigue" is a malady that can afflict us all, for the world has great needs. We may become weary and feel overwhelmed by the enormity of them. But mourning for the world's needs can also bring us again to acknowledge our poverty of spirit. We cannot meet our own needs, nor can we meet all of the world's needs. This realization drives us back to God, whose will is ever directed to the healing of this world that God created and loves. Bumping up against our limits reminds us that we are merely servants. The salvation of the world does not depend on us; it depends on God—who has been working on this salvation since before we came to be and will continue to work on it "until the day of Jesus Christ" (Phil. 1:6, KJV).

EMBODYING GOD'S COMPASSION

So does this mean that only caring inwardly is required of us—that we never actually have to do anything? Of course not. The apostle Paul wrote that we who believe are the body of Christ. We are meant to embody Christ's healing love. In the sixteenth century Teresa of Avila said:

> Christ has . . . no hands but yours, . . .
> Yours are the eyes through which the compassion
>   of Christ is to look out on a hurting world.

When I said earlier that the dark night of our pain offers us a new awareness of God's care, I said we *can* meet God, not that we all *will*. Some people yearn to experience the presence of God in their lives but have no clear sense of God's love and care for them. I understand why. Sensate creatures that we are, we sometimes are limited in grasping truths about God because nothing we can see or hear or touch conveys that truth. We cannot believe that God loves us until another person loves us; we cannot believe that God accepts us until another person accepts us. We cannot believe that God cares when we cry until another person cares for us as we cry. This beatitude contains a call to embody God's steady compassion and accepting presence—not for the entire world, but for the part of the world right in front of us. Through our actions, God can comfort those who mourn. When God's people surround a grieving family, when God's people show up after a disaster to help people rebuild their lives, when we work with abused children or battered women, we prove the truth of this beatitude. We become the embodied truth that God comforts those who mourn. Martin Marty wrote an article for *The Christian Century* years ago discussing what he called "the theology of the casserole." After the death of his wife, many people brought food to his home. Marty wrote of his own former tendency to dismiss such small hospitable acts, denying that they were an expression of any serious theological point. But as he found himself facing, handling, and eating the casseroles brought by loving people, he felt nourished on more than the physical level by these tangible expressions of people's care. Through them he sensed God's sustaining presence.

Second Corinthians tells us that "the God of all comfort . . . comforts us in all our troubles, so *that* we can comfort those in any trouble with the comfort we ourselves have received from God" (2 Cor. 1:3-4, NIV, italics added). As with all the other good gifts that flow into our lives, God's comfort comes to us to be shared and multiplied so *that,* in this new community that Christ brings, no one will be left uncomforted.

Deciding to allow our hearts to be tender and to remain tender is the daily challenge in this beatitude. We can ask God to open our eyes to the joy and the pain around us and to help us see how we are to respond. God invites us to savor life, to be authentic and aware. Instead of rushing through the day, captive to schedules and personal agendas, we can allow ourselves to feel. We can pause in ordinary days to see where mourning exists and to experience the blessedness of God's comfort—given to us or received through us.

DAILY REFLECTIONS FOR WEEK 2

Day 1—Read Ecclesiastes 3:1-11.

Which of the times mentioned in verses 1-8 most resembles your life right now? What "time" is it in your life? What causes you to say this?

Do you think these verses (1-8) are true of most everyone's life? Or in your experience, do some people seem to have mostly good things happen to them, as if they are exempt from life's struggles?

Verse 11 says that God "has made everything suitable for its time." Looking back on struggles and losses in your life, do you see any good that has come from them? Did those times bring anything worthwhile?

Day 2—Read Romans 12:15.

Are you better at weeping with those who weep or at rejoicing with those who rejoice? Why do you think this is so?

Have you ever had someone cry with you over some happening in your life? Have you cried with anyone? What effect does that experience have on a relationship?

How has your congregation recently "wept with" someone who is suffering? What attention does that person still need?

What situations in your life make you rejoice? Who shares your joy?

Day 3—Read John 11:17-36.

Some people think that Christians should not grieve because doing so shows a lack of faith. What does this story offer us when we grieve?

This passage mentions people consoling Mary and Martha. Does your congregation have people who seem to have a gift for helping those who grieve? Are you one of those people? If so, why do you think you are like that? Where or from whom did you learn you learn your response to loss?

What models and responses does this passage offer us as communities of faith for helping someone in grief?

Day 4—Read Isaiah 25:6-9 and 60:19-20 and Revelation 21:1-4.

Envision God tenderly wiping away your tears. What response does this evoke in you—what feelings, memories, hopes?

From the time of Isaiah until John's revelation, prophets have viewed an end to mourning as a part of what God wants. Which of the other differences described in this passage most appeals to you, and why?

Why do you think mourning will not end until we reach the new Jerusalem? Why do mourning and death continue as part of our lives?

Day 5—Read 2 Corinthians 1:3-5.

How does God console us in our afflictions? How has God consoled you?

If all comfort or consolation comes from God, why do some people not feel comforted in difficult times?

What have you learned through your times of suffering and loss that has enabled you to help others in ways that you could not or did not before?

Rewriting the Beatitude

Write here your restatement of this week's beatitude and an opposite "Cursed are . . ." or "Woe to . . ." statement:

Positive: _____ are those who

_____

_____.

Negative:

_____

_____.

Notes for Group Session

My response to this week's beatitude will be

_____

_____.

Power under God's Control

Blessed are the meek, for they will inherit the earth.
—MATTHEW 5:5

You know, I don't think I've ever said, 'Gee, I hope my kids grow up to be meek,' or, 'I've tried really hard to teach my kids to be meek,'" said one person in our small group. We were talking about this beatitude, and when she said that, we laughed. As we tried to come up with images for meekness, we mentioned the proverbial doormat that none of us wants to be; the comic-strip character Caspar Milquetoast, whose name has become a synonym for spinelessness; someone who walks with eyes averted and head down; the television commercial where children say, "I want to grow up to work in a dead-end job," "I want to grow up to be unappreciated and exploited," "I want to live my entire life in obscurity," and so on. None of the images we listed was positive. As in the first two beatitudes, Jesus' words in this third beatitude run counter to our usual perception. Meekness does not seem to be a "blessed" state. And the word *meek* has few positive connotations, if the discussion in our group reflects general attitudes, which I think it does.

There's a reason for that. The Greek word translated "meek" in this passage also carries the meanings of being humble and gentle; and our culture does not reward meekness, gentleness, and humility. Our national self-image (if such a thing is possible) is that we are rugged individualists, fighters with plenty of grit, destined to be leaders of the world. Anyone can make it in America, as the latest self-made millionaires eagerly tell us in interviews—anyone who is willing to work hard and can come up with a good promotional strategy. We like people who speak up, who get things done, who are tough-minded, who do not blink in the face of opposition, who "take the bull by the horns." We like people who can "make the hard decisions" to fire people and close unproductive factories. We are into power, not humility. Even the remote controls for our TVs, stereos, and DVD players don't have on/off buttons; they have power switches. That way, every time we punch one, we are doing much more than simply sending an electrical signal; we are exercising our power!

WHAT THE BIBLE SAYS

Those are cultural norms, not tenets of our faith. Shouldn't our faith help us see meekness more positively? When we consider the comment about meekness not being a quality we try to instill in children, we may question why we have so few positive images for meekness and hear so little about it as believers. One reason may be that the Bible does not examine the qualities of meekness and gentleness in depth. In the King James Version of the Old Testament the words *meek* and *meekness* are used only fifteen times. *Meek* is used only four times in the New Testament, while *meekness* appears twelve times. The words *gentle* and *gentleness* appear only nine times in both testaments combined. (In contrast, words with the root *war—wars, warrior, warring, warfare, warred, warreth*— occur more than 250 times in the Bible.) Words like *humble* and *humility* and their related forms occur more often than *meek* and its cognates, but in general these three character qualities—meekness, gentleness, and humility—don't get much time in the spotlight.

Being humble or meek indicates subjection to a greater power. Numbers 12:3 describes Moses, one of the heroes of Hebrew scripture, as "very humble, more so than anyone else on the face of the earth." Yet Moses faced down the pharaoh of Egypt and led God's people out of Egypt. This is not a picture of a powerless wimp, and it suggests that our understanding of meekness may be incomplete. Moses enjoyed a special relationship with God. The book of Numbers tells us that God comes to prophets in dreams and visions—symbolic communications that are open to many interpretations, confusing and multilevel in meaning. But of Moses God says, "With him I speak face to face, clearly and not in riddles; he sees the form of the LORD" (Num. 12:18, NIV). What an amazing statement to make about someone who is "very humble"! Being privileged to behold the form of God would seem like license to have a fairly high opinion of oneself, but that is not the effect the experience apparently has on Moses. And this may be key to understanding what it means to be meek: to see oneself in relationship to God and God's call—and to realize God's greatness.

Meekness is not low self-esteem or false humility. To see this, we can look again at Moses. He knew himself as called by God to be a leader. Before becoming the leader of the Hebrews, he had been a part of the pharaoh's household. He was able to confront Pharaoh, and that required self-possession and confidence. This guy was no spineless pushover, no colorless, idea-less lump. Rather, Moses was a charismatic, compelling presence who unified the Hebrew slaves and convinced them to follow him out of Egypt. Even so, having encountered God first in the burning bush and then on the mountain, Moses saw his own weaknesses accurately too, and he chose to subject himself to God.

IMAGES OF MEEKNESS

Though it may not seem flattering, one image for meekness is the way horses are trained. When a horse allows itself to be saddled and ridden and directed by a rider, it is said to be "gentled." To gentle a horse is to establish a relationship where the horse's power is used under a human's direction. The horse's power is not taken away. It is still a horse, and horses are powerful creatures. But they can also be as gentle as Danny, a farm horse I know. When my friend Lex was less than two years old, he could ride on Danny's back in perfect safety and relaxation. Danny works with the farmer who owns him (Lex's dad), using his strength and speed to help the farmer with daily tasks. This gentled horse offers me a picture of meekness—power under control.

Another of Jesus' sayings in the fifth chapter of Matthew (v. 41) provides an example of how meekness can be a kind of power. Jesus tells his followers, "If anyone forces you to go one mile, go also the second mile." The country was occupied by Rome, to which the Jewish people paid taxes. We know the attitude of natives toward occupying military forces. At any time Romans could stop Jewish citizens and order them to carry their packs. The law required them to carry this load for one mile only, but Jesus told them to do more—to carry the load a second mile. Imagine that. And who does this put in control? By responding meekly and assuming responsibility for how and when they used their powers, Jesus' followers became free.

But becoming meek is not a once-and-for-all achievement like learning to roller skate or to ride a bike. It is a spiritual decision and a spiritual discipline to which we must continually recommit ourselves. Moses continued to struggle as he led God's people in the wilderness. He still faced self-doubt, anger at God, temptation to use his powers in ways God told him not to (as evidenced in his striking a rock to get water rather than holding his staff over it), and rebellion among the Hebrews.

One challenge of the spiritual life is learning how to place our powers continually under God's control. And we all do have powers—intelligence, skills, energy, for example. We have tongues (I struggle daily with allowing God to direct how I use that power in my life) and emotions such as anger that we can use either to lash out at people or to confront and change unjust systems. Our behavior depends on whether we allow God to direct us. Meekness includes acknowledging our powers while placing them at God's disposal. Meekness is strength under God's control; it is being "gentled" by God, to God's purposes. It is seeing ourselves rightly—not as more than we are (that's arrogance) nor as less (that's false humility).

I make a distinction between being meek toward God and meek toward people. The two are not the same. Moses did not necessarily behave meekly toward people. He did not subject himself to Pharaoh when what Pharaoh asked was wrong, and he confronted Pharaoh when Pharaoh did not keep their agreement. When Jesus overturned the tables of the money changers who were making God's house into "a den of robbers" rather than honoring it as a house of prayer, he was not being meek toward people. Meek people are those who choose to use their powers for God's purposes, at God's time, under God's direction, and who can refrain from using their powers for other ends.

That sounds simple, but it can be quite difficult. All of us are faced with many requests to use our time, energy, money—our powers—and saying no can make people angry with us. Even saying no to ourselves can be tough. Think about how hard it can be to not spend money or to refrain from using a charge card when we see something in a store that we want. (Forget "need"—most of us already have more food, clothing, and "toys" than we need.) Middle-class people in the United States may have difficulty understanding what it means to subject ourselves to God. It may be almost impossible for us. If we have the power to do something or to buy something, why should we hold back? If we want it, we take it. If we want to do it, we go for it.

POWER: TO USE OR NOT TO USE?

Our culture does not help us learn how to wait for gratification of our wishes. In fact, it doesn't teach us much about self-control in any area. The comedy *Real Genius*, a really juvenile (in many ways) movie that I like, tells the story of several highly intelligent, peacenik college students. Their apparently disparate, assigned research projects are actually components of a secret military weapon that will be assembled once their work is complete. Laslo, the most eccentric of the geniuses, figures out what's going on and tells the others. Another character tries to reassure them that the weapon won't be used, since the country is not at war. Laslo responds, "Of course it will! Think about it. There's never been a weapon developed that wasn't used." Cannons, machine guns, the atomic bomb, chemical weapons—they've all been used. All sorts of secret surveillance devices have been used.

We don't do well with refraining from use of our powers. Even the cell phones that many of us intended "for emergencies" we eventually find ourselves using all the time. It is tough to hold our tongue, to dismantle weapons, to choose restraint when retaliation gets more points with the public. It is tough not to seek revenge and not to answer anger with anger. We now have road rage, air rage, even checkout-line rage. (I heard a news item about a woman getting arrested for beating another customer who took thirteen items into a twelve-items-or-fewer checkout lane.) Meekness may seem an impossibly high standard in these days when assertiveness often deteriorates into violence.

Yet this situation is not new. When Jesus said, "Blessed are the meek, for they will inherit the earth," he was quoting directly from Psalm 37. The context of these words in the psalm is waiting for God to act. Five times in this psalm—in verses 9, 11, 22, 29, and 34—God's people are reminded that those who wait for God to vindicate them (rather than taking matters into their own hands) will see God's salvation. It is clear from this psalm and from many other stories in the Bible that retaliation and violence are not God's way. As Romans 12 tells us, vengeance belongs to God, not to us. And repeatedly the Bible reassures us that God will act. Our deciding not to act is often the way of wisdom and of obedience to God.

Think about this in relation to Jesus. In one instance, Jesus drove demons into a herd of pigs who then plunged over a cliff—an act that showed his power and certainly drew attention to him. Yet on another occasion, after proclaiming with authority in the synagogue that God had anointed him to bring healing and good news, he quietly slipped away from the angry crowd and left town, refusing to use his power to protect himself (Luke 4:18-30). While being tempted by the devil in the wilderness, Jesus could have used his power—but he did not. Instead, he quoted scripture (see Matt. 4:1-11). Repeatedly during Jesus' ministry, when skeptics challenged him to give them a sign, to perform this or that miracle to prove his claims, he refused. When confronted in the garden of Gethsemane by soldiers there to arrest him, he told his disciples that God would put "twelve legions of angels" at his disposal if he asked—but he chose instead to allow himself to be arrested (Matt. 26:53). He subjected himself and his power to God.

Meekness is choosing to refrain from exercising our power, refusing to answer power with power. An employee doing what the boss wants, a teenager obeying parents—these persons make themselves subject to another. Wisdom distinguishes between times to take action and times to restrain ourselves in using the powers at our disposal. We don't have to prove anything by doing everything we could do. In fact, sometimes saying yes to God's call may require us to say no to other offers that look attractive and may even be good acts in themselves. If they are not what God wants for us, accepting them is disobedience.

In a culture obsessed with who owns the most, who earns the most money or degrees, who scores the most points, who swims or skis or runs or drives the fastest, the idea of choosing to do less than we might is foreign. Choosing not to act is not spectacular; and for many of us, it is not easy. Yet, this beatitude tells us, those who choose not to fight and not to strive for ascendancy over others are the ones who will inherit the earth. The meek are those who renounce power and competition as ways of dealing with people and winning approval. We don't have to strain, flex our muscles, and show off our strength to earn our inheritance. Inheritances come because of the heirs' relationship to the giver, not because of what the heirs do. Inheriting the earth is not like the Sooner land rush in Oklahoma; it's not a matter of running faster than others to stake out a claim. We inherit the earth because we submit ourselves to God. For me, this beatitude is mirrored in the admonition "Humble yourselves before the Lord, and he will exalt you" (James 4:10). Psalm 44:6-7 says, "Not in my bow do I trust, nor can my sword save me. But you [God] have saved us."

SUBVERSIVE SPIRITUALITY

Remember who Jesus was talking to when he spoke about inheriting the earth. His audience was the people of Israel, who had been nomads. These were the people who had been the wandering *habiru*—the Hebrews, whose very name meant wanderer—people without a land to call their own. God promised them that they would possess a land "flowing with milk and honey" (Exod. 3:8). Milk meant dairy herds and honey meant beehives, and these possessions meant having a land to call home, being settled. For the Israelites, having a land meant seeing God's promise fulfilled. God had said through the prophets that they would be a nation, so talk about inheriting the earth would be close to their hearts. But the Israelites had not gotten their land by being meek. You may remember the stories of how the Hebrews entered Canaan and conquered the Hittites and the Hivites and the Jebusites and the Per-izzites and all the other -ites. Some of the stories present harsh pictures of war and mass executions, and the people listening to Jesus knew this history. So meekness as a means to inheriting the earth would have seemed to them a surprising and subversive sort of spirituality.

Meekness remains subversive. For many of us, the Western ideal of productivity and upward mobility has permeated even our ideas about serving God. We say that numbers in churches don't count, but the pastors people listen to and invite to speak at the big conferences are the ones with the big congregations. I have a friend, someone I have known since childhood, who is a pastor. An intelligent man, he did well in seminary, maintaining a high grade-point average even while pastoring as a student. The leaders of his denomination "had their eyes on him," as the saying goes. He was an up-and-comer. His first pastorate was in a fairly small congregation. Over a period of a few years, the congregation grew modestly, and he enjoyed building relationships with the people. He is a good preacher, but what he most loves is teaching the Bible and guiding people spiritually. Soon the leaders of his denomination approached him to talk with him about moving to a larger church that was searching for a pastor. He declined, saying he was doing well where he was. Having built a level of trust with his parishioners, he felt that his greatest effectiveness in guiding them still lay ahead. The next year and the next, he was told about and then finally urged to consider other, larger churches, for the good of his career. As he and his wife and I talked about this during a visit, he said, "I don't need a larger church. I am doing what God called me to do, and this number of people is just about right. If I go to a church with more people, I won't have time to be a pastor to them in the way they need a pastor. Can't they understand that I want to stay here?" They couldn't. The ruling paradigm was upward mobility, which meant a bigger church with more people, more money, more prestige. Yes, he had the abilities and skills to administer the activities of a larger congregation, but he didn't feel a need to move to progressively larger churches. He felt he was doing what God had called him to do, right where he was. Why should he leave that place of ministry?

Moving would not necessarily have been a bad thing, but my friend did not feel it was right for him. Hearing of his struggle with his superiors' expectations taught me about the importance of evaluating opportunities and requests. So much good could be done. Think of all the opportunities in your congregation. I belong to a large church that offers many more opportunities to serve God through its ministries than I could ever take advantage of. I could easily stay busy all the time, doing good things in God's name. It would be possible to be a full-time volunteer through my church. I could stay so busy that I had little time for prayer, reflection, journaling—for listening to God's specific call to me about where I am to use my powers. I believe God calls everyone to do something—but God doesn't call anyone to do everything. And only God can tell me which opportunities are *my* opportunities, the ones where I am to use my powers—to do good or to take action to restrain evil.

WAITING TO HEAR GOD

To be meek toward God means being willing to submit myself to God. But how can I submit myself to God's call if I do not have time to listen for it? The truth is, so much needs to be done that if we hesitate, someone will certainly give us a task to do "for God." That this task may not be what God is calling me to do may never occur to those who ask. After all, they are not in charge of whether I submit myself to God. Those who call on me are busy doing what they feel is God's work for them, and if they are recruiting badly needed workers, they are unlikely to ask me, "Now, have you prayed about this? Are you sure this is God's will for you right now? Is this how God wants you to use your time and energy?" If I meekly agreed to do everything I am asked to do, I might be—no, I would be—too busy (and too tired) to respond to God's primary call on my life.

Answering that call begins not with activity but with waiting on God. This brings us back to Psalm 37, which enjoins the meek to wait for God and promises that those who do this "shall inherit the earth" (v. 9, KJV). Jesus said to the disciples when they wanted to use force in the garden of Gethsemane, "All who draw the sword shall die by the sword" (Matt. 26:52, NIV). Those who choose to answer violence with violence, power with power, will have to continue using their power against one another. Left to that pattern, the bellicose types will eventually kill one another. Only those who refuse to enter the competition will be left standing when the power struggles are over—and God will use those who have learned meekness to establish a different kind of world. In God's peaceable kingdom, on God's holy mountain, according to Isaiah's vision, even the animals will no longer hurt or destroy one another. The leopard will lie down with the kid, and the young child will play in safety near the adder (Isa. 11:6-9). All of their powers will be subject to God's holy will, and they will serve one another in love. Peace will characterize God's new kingdom where the meek are in charge of the earth.

We face choices daily about how to use our energy. As Paul wrote to the Corinthians, "By the meekness and gentleness of Christ, I appeal to you. . . . Though we live in the world, we do not wage war as the world does. The weapons we fight with are not the weapons of the world. On the contrary, they have divine power to demolish strongholds. We demolish arguments and every pretension that sets itself up against the knowledge of God, and we take captive every thought to make it obedient to Christ" (2 Cor. 10:1, 3-5, NIV). Committing ourselves to listening for God's direction means committing ourselves to being selective in responding to the invitations that come to us.

Sometimes saying no is the faithful and meek response that honors God's call. As Jesus said in this beatitude, those who place their powers at God's disposal, who allow the Spirit to "gentle" them, will inherit God's kingdom.

Daily Reflections for Week 3

Day 1—Read Psalm 37:7-11, 32-34.

According to this psalm, what are the behaviors and attitudes of the righteous in contrast to the wicked?

What do you think it would look like to "wait for the Lord" in the sense that this psalm describes?

When are you tempted to fret about those who seem not to care about God, even openly oppose God, and yet prosper? What people and activities unsettle you and cause you to wonder about justice and fairness?

How do you think the world would be different if the meek were in charge? Do you think you'd like them to be? Why or why not?

Day 2—Read Romans 12:17-21.

"Revenge is sweet," the saying goes. How does that saying compare with the message of this passage?

How does the advice given in this passage compare to our culture's norms? How does it compare to what we see in action movies and in reality television shows?

What might happen if you tried the strategy of doing good to one of your enemies? What would it take to get you to try this?

When have you returned evil for evil, perhaps with a sibling? What usually happens when we try this strategy?

Day 3—Read Matthew 5:38-47.

Jesus' words about turning the other cheek are familiar to many of us. What would your coworkers or fellow church members think of a person who publicly "turned the other cheek" to someone who was mistreating him or her? How does this strategy appeal to you?

How can we apply Jesus' words in this passage to our usual encounters? Do you think Jesus really meant we should lend money to anyone who asks?

Have you ever prayed over an extended period of time for someone you consider an enemy? If so, what happened? If not, how do you feel about considering that course of action?

Some people think that we should not have enemies, but Jesus talks about them in many places in the Gospels. What does this say to you about having enemies and about Jesus?

Day 4—Read Romans 14:1-21.

About what issues (example: drinking, political protest marches, war and peace, abortion) do your opinions differ from others' in your community of faith? What does this passage suggest about such differences?

Those who allow more latitude in personal practice are called "the strong ones" in this passage, but they are also told not to exercise their liberty, not to do what might offend others. What do you think of this advice?

Have you ever chosen not to do something you really wanted to do (and felt was morally acceptable), so you wouldn't upset another believer? How did you feel, or how do you think you would feel, in that situation?

This passage seems to say we should live by the standards of the most cautious among us. How might subjecting ourselves to other believers express meekness? How do you decide when to speak out for what you believe and for what needs to change, and when to remain silent?

Day 5—Read Matthew 4:1-11.

What powers did "the tempter" ask Jesus to use? How did Jesus respond?

The tempter came to Jesus when Jesus was hungry and therefore vulnerable. He asked Jesus to use his powers in ways God did not intend. Which of your powers are you most often tempted to misuse? In what situations are you vulnerable to misusing them?

Rewriting the Beatitude

Write here your restatement of this week's beatitude and an opposite "Cursed are . . ." or "Woe to . . ." statement. For some biblical suggestions about the opposite of this beatitude, reread Psalm 37.

Positive: _____ are those who

_____

_____.

Negative:

_____

_____.

Notes for Group Session

My response to this week's beatitude will be

_____

_____.

Satisfied with Being Unsatisfied

**Blessed are those who hunger and thirst for righteousness,
for they will be filled.**

—MATTHEW 5:6

Minutes passed as I inched along in bumper-to-bumper traffic on the interstate entrance ramp. Deep in thought about work issues I had just left behind, I gradually became aware that I was uncomfortable. What was bothering me? Where was the discomfort? It was something physical. But what was it? My stomach? Yes, definitely my stomach. What was wrong with my stomach? Turning my attention to the gnawing, I realized that I was hungry. Very hungry. That was it. But why was I so hungry that my stomach was interrupting my thoughts? Looking back over the day, I remembered I had worked through lunch. But I do that sometimes, and I usually didn't feel this hungry even after skipping lunch. Going back further, I realized I hadn't eaten breakfast either. In fact, I hadn't eaten since dinner the night before! Knowing something about human biology, I figured my stomach had probably been trying for a while to get my attention and tell me that I needed to eat—but obviously I had been tuning out its pleas.

You may not believe it's possible to forget to eat. But for me it is. On that day, years ago, I had rushed to get my daughter to school on time that morning and then to make the first of a daylong series of meetings. Between meetings, I had returned phone calls and made sure things in the office were moving along as they needed to be. I had worked through the lunch hour to get ready for the afternoon, and food simply had not crossed my mind. Other matters had seemed more pressing, or I had apparently decided they were more pressing. I can tune out my hungers.

And I used to be not much better at heeding my thirst. But I discovered by accident that my body needs water and will tell me so—again, if I pay attention. You've probably heard the medical guideline that we should drink six to eight glasses of water a day. I happen to like water, but I wasn't deliberate about drinking it until I joined a weight-loss group. There I was urged to drink lots of water because it would both help with weight loss and hydrate my skin. So I decided to give it a try. Over a period of time, drinking water became a habit; and I began drinking water because I found myself craving it. My body learned the good feeling of getting enough water, and I learned to recognize when I was thirsty. I also discovered that many times when I'd reached for a snack, I had really been wanting water. How could I be so out of touch with my basic needs for food and water? I'm just so busy with life that I forget to attend to my body's gentle nudgings. I think something similar is true of many of us spiritually.

There's a *Peanuts* cartoon in which Charlie Brown begins a letter to his pen pal by saying, "I would have written sooner, but I forgot about you." Many of us could begin a letter to our spiritual selves with those words. Sometimes we live as if our spiritual self were a pen pal in some faraway country—sending an occasional report when we have time or are bored or when an unusual event happens in our lives. In between, we may almost forget that we have a spiritual self. Our culture makes it possible for us to keep our lives so busy that we can ignore spiritual hunger and thirst. We can entertain ourselves or exercise ourselves or work ourselves so hard that we do not heed little nudgings of our spirit and of the Holy Spirit. Though our calendars may be full to overflowing, we can remain empty and unsatisfied at the deepest levels of our being.

I can see why Jesus said that those who hunger and thirst for righteousness are blessed. Hungering and thirsting for righteousness means being aware that more exists than our eyes see, than our bodies need. It means knowing that we need a relationship with God and recognizing that time spent with God feeds us. It means hungering for something better than the status quo. That word, *righteousness,* is a good one to use in naming our deepest longings. The word Jesus used means "rightness," "fairness," "to be in right relationship with God and other people." Those who "hunger and thirst for righteousness" want to be right in character and action. Those who are righteous are doing things rightly—as they ought to be done. They are in the right in what they do, what they say, what they love. To open ourselves to God and acknowledge our hunger for righteousness, therefore, means opening ourselves to be changed, to have our affections and our actions changed. When we are disappointed in ourselves for our inability to be better and to do better, we are feeling our hunger and thirst for righteousness. In fact, I believe that all our vague, unsatisfied, and unsatisfiable yearnings are in some way at their root the yearning to know God, to be put right with God, and to see the world put right with God. Just as our physical hunger and thirst remind us that we are made to eat and drink, our hunger for meaning and direction in life reminds us that we are created to need and want God—continually, even if we have not yet put a name on the yearning—and to serve God. Sometimes I find myself standing before the refrigerator with the door open, scanning the shelves, hungry for something even though I can't say what. That vague, gnawing awareness has a spiritual parallel in our restlessness, even our discomfort, with our lives as they are.

The word of grace for us in all this is Christ's assurance that we "will be filled," that God has already begun responding to our hunger and thirst, even before we know they exist. The fifteenth-century philosopher Blaise Pascal said that there is a God-shaped void within each of us; Augustine said that our hearts are restless until they find rest in God. God already seeks us and from the beginning of time has sought us to answer the yearnings of our hearts. Paul wrote to the Romans that while we were still dead in sin, unaware of our need for God, Christ came. In Wesleyan terms, God's grace at work in us is the force that helps us become aware that we hunger and thirst. Thinking in these terms, I can see why Jesus said those who hunger and thirst for righteousness are "blessed." Realizing that we are spiritually hungry proves that God is working within us.

Awareness of our need for God is basic to the spiritual life. (As the first beatitude tells us, it is the door into the kingdom of God.) Hunger and thirst for God are as continual and as much a part of us as our physical needs. In fact, Luke's version of this beatitude (6:21) says simply that those who hunger will be filled, making no distinction between physical and spiritual hungers. Some commentators say that Luke's love and concern for the poor and the outcast caused him to word this beatitude as a statement about the radical nature of God's new kingdom: Luke was calling for a new social order and redistribution of wealth so that all would have their needs met. But Luke's version can also remind us that spiritual hungers are meant to be considered as important as physical hungers.

Of course, being human, we are tempted to quantify. We often try to reduce all our spiritual hungers to a specific diet that tells us exactly what to do, as we do with weight-control or cholesterol-reducing or sugar-avoiding diets. Various diet programs have made millions for their creators. That happens for at least two reasons: (1) because people want someone to make weight control easy for them, to give them clear direction about how to achieve results; and (2) because the different diets do work for different people. But just as no single diet is right for all bodies, no single spiritual diet is right for all spirits. The spiritual life cannot be reduced to one simple set of rules.

Jesus said that over and over, in a variety of ways. But we tend to drift into rigid patterns for "doing" spirituality. Having a clear plan and stated goals comforts us. These give us something to measure ourselves by, a way to know we're doing okay, that we're at least "in the ballpark"—whatever the game. We love self-assessment quizzes in magazines; we love top-ten lists. We even look at lists like these Beatitudes and want to rate ourselves on how we're doing—in poverty of spirit I'm about a 5; in mourning I'm not doing so well—a 2, maybe; in meekness, I'm doing really great—at least a 7. Or we congratulate ourselves because we're reading the Bible five days out of seven—a lot better than last year. We want to know we're making progress, so we need things we can count and track. But righteousness is about being in right relationship—and relationship cannot be reduced to a neat formula.

Most of us who have spent time in church have heard about lots of strategies for growing in the spiritual life, strategies that have worked for lots of people. (As with diets, that's why they get written down and circulated.) But each of us has a unique relationship with God, with unique hungers and thirsts. My hungers and preferences in foods are unique to me, just as yours are to you. I don't like pickle-and-peanut-butter sandwiches, but some people really love them. That's fine. As the saying goes, one person's meat is another one's poison. What feeds me and helps me grow spiritually may bore another person to glassy-eyed catatonia; what energizes you may overwhelm me. And that makes it hard. We want someone to tell us how to do the spiritual life. We want someone to solve the puzzle for us, to give us the formula, to draw the picture. Some of us live with enormous guilt about our inability to get the spiritual life "right."

Getting in touch with our personal hunger and thirst for God, for our unique relationship with God, may require us to adjust our boundaries. Years ago, I worried a lot about my daughter's eating—or lack of interest in eating, I should say. Then I read a book by Virginia Ramey Mollenkott, one of a series of books where religious leaders told their personal stories of coming to faith. In the book, *Speech, Silence, Action!: The Cycle of Faith,* Mollenkott told about her own journey toward loving and accepting herself as a large woman who would never have the svelte figure our culture approves. She included a chart of ten "eating styles," showing sets of eating preferences that make different people feel energetic, well, and satisfied. That chart opened my eyes to understand a repeated, daily struggle I had been having with my daughter. She and I have different eating styles—I could immediately spot mine and then hers in the chart. Seeing that what constitutes a healthy diet varies from person to person set me free from worrying so much about what did or did not get eaten. It also dramatically changed the atmosphere at our dinner table. This insight enabled me to change my intensity about the "shoulds" and "oughts" I had been imposing, from the very best of motives, on my child.

Sometimes we seem to do something similar regarding the spiritual life, adopting a one-size-fits-all paradigm of the spiritual disciplines that we all "ought" to live by. Without meaning to, we may adopt the idea (and convey to others) that we should all pray in this way, for this long, about these things, in this order; read this much of the Bible; give this much time each week; journal every day; and _____ (add here your own personal practice that you feel guilty about not doing or not doing well enough). This approach has caused many of us to give up on ever being "righteous," to live in honest and loving relationship with God— because, when we're honest, we have to admit that much of what is called holy lies beyond our grasp. We don't enjoy it; it doesn't feed us. We may even decide that we don't really "hunger and thirst for righteousness" because we don't enjoy keeping some particular set of rules about following God that we've read or heard about. But as I said before, relationship with God is not a matter of rules. God invites us, instead, into an open-ended relationship. That prospect can terrify us. Where might we end up if we were to recognize our spiritual hungers and decide to let God feed us? For some of us, to commit ourselves to a journey whose end we cannot predict and whose route we will not see in advance requires moving our boundaries a great distance. What Jesus said to his hearers reassures us: God acts in response to our hungers, our yearning.

We, the well-fed and well-watered, may be unable to hear the enormity of the promise in this beatitude for those who first heard Jesus say, "Blessed are those who hunger and thirst. . . ." These people lived in an agrarian society, their lives intimately tied to nature. They grew their food or hunted or fished the land and waters around them. Drought meant possible starvation; excess rain meant seeds rotting in the ground—again, possible starvation. Theirs was a precarious existence. They lived on the edge of the desert, in constant risk of thirst and famine. This promise that God would feed them spiritually and satisfy their thirst for righteousness surely must have reminded them of their daily struggles and seemed incredible. But Jesus said God would respond, and that remains true.

Until we recognize our inner gnawing as spiritual hunger, we try to live on hors d'oeuvres and salt water, not understanding why we only seem thirstier and less satisfied than before. But our hope to have our yearnings satisfied rests on the faithfulness of God whom we hunger to know, the One who has been seeking us all our lives. God designed our spiritual hunger and thirst into us; they are a part of the original specifications for being fully human.

We are created for relationship with God, and nothing else can satisfy that longing. We are created with a desire to see the people of the world living in right relationship with God and one another. (Listen to any group of first graders declaring, "But that's not fair!" for evidence of this.) We may ignore our hungers or try to satisfy them by a thousand means other than turning to God. We may keep our calendars so full that we don't have time to ask ourselves if we are deeply happy, if life has meaning. But that will not make the hungers go away. They are a permanent part of us at the deepest level of our being. As we recognize our hunger and thirst, God draws each of us into an individually unique relationship that is life's greatest adventure. To heed our longing for God and for transformation of ourselves and the world is to be deeply blessed.

DAILY REFLECTIONS FOR WEEK 4

Day 1—Read Psalm 63:1-8.

In what settings are you most likely to become aware of your hunger and thirst to know God, to be with God? How does this hunger feel?

What feeds you spiritually? What renews you and strengthens your commitment to being God's person?

The psalmist says, "My soul clings to you." What image or images would you use to describe your feeling of hunger for and closeness to God?

Day 2—Read Isaiah 55:1-4.

This passage makes clear that some "foods" nourish the soul, and some do not. What activities in the community of faith have you done or tried to do that left you feeling unsatisfied? What do you wish you felt that you do not?

In what activities have you participated that became rich food for your soul and spirit?

This passage calls out to those who know they are thirsty and hungry. What awakens people to their hunger for God? What causes them to begin to look for something more than just getting by day to day? What causes you to?

Day 3—Read 1 Kings 18:36–19:10.

What cycles are you aware of in your spiritual life? What nudges you to renew your interest during "down" times?

What would you say to a friend who feels like Elijah did, alone and besieged by life?

God sent an angel to feed Elijah when he was feeling overwhelmed and tempted to give up. What "angels" have come to you in a time of depression or loss of interest in your faith? What did they do that fed you and helped you begin to talk with God again?

Day 4—Read John 4:1-30, 39-42.

If Jesus were standing before you, what questions would you want to ask about serving God? How do you think he would answer you?

This woman asked Jesus about right ways and wrong ways and places to worship. What ways of worshiping are you most comfortable with? What ways of worshiping make you uncomfortable? What do you think Jesus would say to you about these ways?

Have you ever had a serious conversation about religion with someone of another faith? What would you like to know about other faiths? Have you ever had a friend of another faith? If so, what did you learn from that friendship? If not, why not?

Day 5—Read John 6:25-40.

How has God most often fed you spiritually? through books and reading? through Bible study? (in groups or alone?) through preaching? through retreats? through your participation in mission projects?

Looking back over your spiritual journey, what has most consistently been life-giving for you? What has helped to renew you as you follow Christ?

Rewriting the Beatitude

Write here your restatement of this week's beatitude and an opposite "Cursed are . . ." or "Woe to . . ." statement:

Positive: _____ are those who

_____

_____.

Negative:

_____

_____.

Notes for Group Session

My response to this week's beatitude will be

_____

_____.

Grace That Acts

Blessed are the merciful, for they will receive mercy.
—Matthew 5:7

This beatitude addresses the first attitude or trait that seems to imply positive action. Three of the four so far—being poor in spirit, mourning, hungering and thirsting—are inward or spiritual and therefore invisible, happening within an individual. The fourth characteristic, meekness, involves submission and sometimes refraining from acting when we could act. So we could "do" the first four beatitudes without that being obvious to anyone and without involving anyone else. Being merciful, however, involves taking positive action to help another. Three of the first four beatitudes concern lack—poverty, loss, hunger and thirst—and the fourth one is about being in subjection. We probably aren't eager to be identified with those states. But most of us wouldn't mind being called merciful; that is a positive word, if being merciful doesn't include being a softie or a pushover.

One definition of *merciful* is "showing kindness in excess of what is deserved." That definition reminds us that mercy involves judgment, since it hinges on what someone "deserves"—and that means evaluation of behavior. When a criminal appeals to the mercy of the court, the appeal implies guilt or at least conviction for a crime. How can we get better than we deserve if no sentence has been set or no evaluation has been done?

IMAGES OF MERCY

Mercy is mentioned more often in scripture than meekness and gentleness, so we have more information on which to build an understanding of it than we do of meekness. One familiar picture of mercy in scripture is the story of Jesus interacting with the woman caught in adultery. Her accusers bring her to Jesus, saying that she has been taken "in the very act" (John 8:4). According to the Law, she should have been or at least could have been stoned—and apparently that is what the crowd of accusers had in mind. (I always picture the woman kneeling, covering her face with her hands in humiliation, having been shoved toward Jesus by those bringing her to be condemned.) As Jesus listens to the woman's accusers, he leans down and begins to write in the sand. This is one of those Bible stories that invites conjecture. What did Jesus write? Did he write the names of some other common sins? Did he write one of the commandments? Did he write the name of the man with whom the woman had been found but who was not being dragged before Jesus as she was? Then Jesus says to those who have brought the woman, "Let anyone among you who is without sin be the first to throw a stone at her" (John 8:7). What could he have written that caused what happened next? In my mind's eye, I see the accusers averting their eyes as Jesus speaks. I see some of them begin to squirm. Then I see one person turn and quietly walk away—and then another, and another, until finally only Jesus and the woman remain. At this point Jesus says to her, "Woman, where are they? Has no one condemned you?" (8:10).

I imagine her looking over her shoulder in surprise, not having realized that the crowd has diminished. Her face changes, the red of her embarrassed blush beginning to fade. She turns back in amazement to say to Jesus, "No one, sir" (8:11).

And Jesus says to her, "Neither do I condemn you. Go your way, and from now on do not sin again" (8:11). Note that Jesus does not dismiss what she has done, saying that it does not matter. He uses the word *sin*, implying that she did what she is accused of. According to Jesus' example, mercy does not explain away troubling behavior, excusing it as if it had not happened or denying its seriousness. On the contrary, mercy acknowledges that wrong has been done and that punishment is justified, but it deals more gently than could be justified by the letter of the law.

Some people have difficulty separating the wrong action from the person, thinking that to condemn the action means we must also condemn the actor and separate ourselves from him or her. I see an example of this in the movie *Dead Man Walking,* which tells the story of a young man who has been convicted of killing a young couple, after raping the woman. This movie is based on a true story. While the man is on death row, he is befriended by a nun, Helen Prejean, who visits him regularly. Slowly, as Prejean builds a relationship with him, she decides also to visit the family of one of his victims, to see how they are coping with their grief and loss. In one scene she stands outside the home of the family, speaking with them through a screen door as she explains who she is. Once invited in, she talks with them about their loss, expressing her concern. Knowing that she has been visiting the man convicted of killing their child, family members are at first reluctant to speak with her. But slowly they begin talking. Finally, the father asks why she has changed her mind about the murderer and turned from him to them. She explains that she is still visiting the convicted man and plans to continue doing so, and the father orders her to leave their home.

The father refuses to speak with anyone who considers the convicted man anything more than an animal, and he cannot accept sympathy from anyone who does not hate the young man on death row as he hates him. He cannot believe that Sister Prejean can simultaneously care about someone convicted of committing murder and about his victim's family. In this father's way of understanding life, she must take sides against the one who has done wrong. For him, seeking justice excludes mercy—as it does for many whose loved ones have been killed.

This attitude underlies one of our concerns about mercy: whether it is possible to be too merciful. What if we show mercy to a criminal, allow the person to go free, and then that person repeats the crime? Are we then guilty of collusion? What if we give a second chance to someone who has hurt us and that person hurts us again? Have we been too merciful? Have we been manipulated? These are difficult questions, to be sure, but Jesus' words to the woman caught in adultery give us a clear model. He names her sin as what it is, and then he tells her clearly to change her behavior in the future—to "go . . . and do not sin again."

WHAT SCRIPTURE SAYS

As we see in these two stories, mercy is not merely feeling sympathy. Mercy is extended by one who has the power to condemn or punish but chooses not to. We choose not to criticize, not to say, "I told you so," not to exact our "pound of flesh"—not to avenge. As Jesus shows us in his interaction with the woman caught in adultery, mercy does not look back at what the person has done but forward to what the person can do in the future. Have you ever been tempted to rehash someone's past misdeeds? Have you ever caught yourself saying to someone in an argument, "This is the same old thing. You've done what you always do . . . "? Most of us have some memories of others' misdeeds that we revisit from time to time. We may even mention them as leverage in current disagreements. Mercy, however, lets go of the past. In this sense mercy could be considered an expression of love, for as 1 Corinthians 13 tells us, love "keeps no record of wrongs" (v. 5, NIV). It lets them go.

Jesus mentioned mercy in denouncing selective attention to what God asks of us. He pointed out that some "tithed" the little things—kept the rules about minor issues that did not require personal change or involvement with another—but neglected the "weightier matters of the law: justice and mercy" (Matt. 23:23). Jesus clearly told us that mercy and judgment are weighty matters.

Why is mercy important? This beatitude gives one reason: because God will show mercy to those who are merciful. If for no other reason than self-interest, we show mercy—in order to receive mercy. And we all need mercy. I've heard people say they're glad God will mete out justice. I'm not eager for justice, at least not for myself. I don't want to get what I deserve. I want a lot better than that; I want kindness in excess of what I deserve. This beatitude says that God will be merciful to me if I am merciful to others. This is important because I often need mercy. One factor that helps me be willing to extend mercy to others is staying in touch with my own capacity to be a jerk. At times I can do and say thoughtless and hurtful things; I can act harshly toward people around me, behaving as if I matter and they do not. I can enforce the rules I agree with, with gusto, caring more about judgment than about the people involved. But Jesus paired judgment with mercy. So how do we balance them? How do we show mercy while doing what must be done?

Looking for the answer to this question brought me to what I believe is a pivotal verse about mercy. The prophet Micah wrote that God has shown us what is good: "To act justly and to love mercy and to walk humbly with . . . God" (Micah 6:8, NIV). This is the key—acting for justice while loving mercy, holding the two in tension. How do we do that?

Again, I find a helpful image in a story about death row, Stephen King's book *The Green Mile*. This book tells the story of a mentally challenged man who is sentenced to death and of the prison officials who watch over him and the others waiting to be executed. Two of the prison employees display dramatically different attitudes toward the work they must do. One of them, who has worked in the prison system for many years, cares about the men in his charge. He takes time as their executions approach to talk with them, to see if there are matters he can care for on their behalf, messages they want to send, things they need to talk about. He finds no pleasure in escorting men to the electric chair or in seeing them die. In fact, he struggles with the task and dreads each death. In stark contrast to him, another guard is a vengeful, hate-filled man. This second guard deliberately botches the execution of a prisoner who has mocked him, making the death even more horrible than it has to be. The first guard, for me, exemplifies someone who cares about both mercy and justice. Though tormented to a degree by his role in what the state said justice required, he still acted lovingly and showed mercy in the ways he could.

How can we sustain that attitude? How can we confront behavior that needs to be changed and remain merciful? The prophet gives us the answer: by walking "humbly with God"—and only by doing this. As we spend time with God and experience the searing light of God's loving holiness, we come to see ourselves as we are: imperfect and deeply stained by our sins, and at the same time deeply loved. That is true for every one of us, convicted murderers and petty thieves and conniving siblings and outwardly "nice" people. None of us can save ourselves or remove the stains of our sins, whatever they are or however small they may be. As the saying goes, "There is so much good in the worst of us and so much bad in the best of us, that it hardly behooves any of us to speak ill of the rest of us." Every person on this earth is a dearly loved child of God for whom Christ died—and each one of us is a sinner in need of grace and mercy.

That is not news, of course. The Jesus Prayer, "Lord Jesus Christ, Son of God, have mercy on me, a sinner," became the breath prayer of a Russian peasant hundreds of years ago, and it remains an appropriate prayer for all of us. We need not just eternal, ultimate mercy but mercy now in our daily life as we interact with others. God has already shown us mercy and grace by awakening our spirits to our need for Christ, and God will deepen our capacity to extend mercy to others.

CHOOSING TO LEARN MERCY

But we have to learn mercy—and not everyone does. Two Bible stories come to mind as illustrations of this truth. The first is the parable of the unforgiving servant, found in Matthew 18. In this parable, a man deeply in debt, owing more than fifteen years' wages, pleads with his creditor for mercy. The creditor agrees and forgives the man his huge debt. The forgiven servant leaves for home and encounters a man who owes him a relatively small amount compared to his own debt—the equivalent of about 100 days' wages. He seizes the man and demands payment, having him thrown in jail when he cannot pay. Though the first man was shown mercy by the one to whom he owed a huge amount, he did not learn from his experience to extend mercy to others.

The contrasting second story is the parable of the good Samaritan. You probably remember hearing about the man who is beaten by thieves and left for dead along a road. A priest passes by and sees the injured man but does not stop to help. Then a Temple employee, a Levite, comes along. He also sees the man but does not stop to help. Finally a Samaritan, one of a group despised by Jews and considered unclean, comes along. Seeing the wounded man, the Samaritan dresses his wounds, takes him to an inn, and when he must leave, pays the innkeeper to continue to care for the man as he recovers. I feel sure that all three men who passed along that road had experienced "kindness in excess of what was deserved" at some times during their lives. But apparently only one of them—the Samaritan—allowed his experiences to soften his heart and teach him compassion toward others.

In our daily interactions with others, we can choose to attend to our lives as a school in showing mercy. Or we can ignore all the ways God's enduring mercy has touched us. We can forget all the times when we've gotten better than we deserve, from God and from other people. Or we can choose to remember those times and draw from them lessons in how we can show others mercy.

Mercy can be a matter of small acts: letting someone into a line of traffic even though they've been driving on the shoulder of the road to get around the backup, taking a lunch to the child who forgot it (and whom you have told, "Next time you'll just have to go hungry or work it out yourself. You have to learn some responsibility!"), giving a chronically late employee one more chance before writing up the lapse again. And mercy is also a matter of great acts, of deciding to forgive someone who has hurt us deeply and changed our life forever.

Like other habits of the heart that we can learn as we listen to God and follow the Holy Spirit's nudges, mercy can become more and more natural to us. As we practice mercy, we enlarge our capacity for it. We can look at this beatitude as an affirmation: as we offer mercy to others, God continually refills us with mercy so that we can experience and extend it on deeper and deeper levels. This view of mercy implies continuing relationship, continuing connection with God ("walk humbly with your God"), where we remain open to be filled with mercy because we continually see our own need for it.

In our daily interactions we have the power to criticize, condemn, and censure others in our words and by our actions. We also have the power to offer mercy, to offer others a chance to see their possibilities for something more, to help them turn from the past and toward the future. God empowers us to choose more than our human nature would prefer—to offer mercy rather than to seek vengeance. Mercy is choosing to use for good whatever power we have. We may not have great power by the world's standards, but we all have spiritual power. The prisoner who has no power to escape still has the power to forgive the executioner even as the blade of the guillotine falls. Mercy is choosing to use our power to extend grace when we could just as well use it to exact punishment. Jesus promised that those who do so will find God's mercy extended to them.

DAILY REFLECTIONS FOR WEEK 5

Day 1—Read James 2:1-13.

When have you received better than you deserved? In what situation did someone show mercy instead of passing judgment on you? How did you respond?

Do you find it easier to be merciful in some situations than in others, toward some kinds of people more than others? For you, what makes the difference between being able to be merciful and not being able to do so? What conditions do you place on your mercy?

James 2 says that if we fail in keeping one of God's commands, we are guilty of disobeying them all, implying that all sins are equal. What sins does our culture consider particularly bad? What sins do we talk most about in our churches? Are some sins more serious than others?

Day 2—Read Matthew 18:23-35.

When has someone come to you and asked forgiveness? How did you respond? Was extending forgiveness possible for you? Was it difficult?

Think of some debt—literal or emotional—that someone owes you, and consider canceling it. How do you think doing so would affect your actions? Does this feel like something you could or should do? Why or why not?

Imagine that you are a friend of the unforgiving servant, going to visit him in jail. What would you want to say to him? What prayer would you offer for him?

Day 3—Read Luke 6:32-38.

In what settings (job, parenting, etc.) do you have responsibility for evaluating others? How do you feel about doing this?

In those settings, is mercy always an option? Or do you operate within policies and procedures that mandate particular responses in certain situations—"zero tolerance" or something similar for some offenses? How can we show mercy even when the rules seem to offer no latitude?

In what areas of your life do you struggle to forgive? Have you made progress toward forgiving, or are you stuck somewhere along the road to forgiveness? Or does forgiving come easily for you? If it does, why do you think you are like this when some people struggle to forgive?

Day 4—Read Romans 9:15-26.

Where in the world do you see injustice today? How do you think God feels about those injustices?

Have you ever wanted to argue with God about the outcome of some situation, such as a wicked person prospering? When has the unfairness of some parts of life bothered you?

Listen to God saying to you, "You once were not mine, but you shall be called 'a child of the living God.'" How does this make you feel? How does your life show that you are a child of God?

Day 5—Read Lamentations 3:21-25.

Verse 23 says God's mercy toward us is "new every morning." Where have you experienced God's mercy recently?

In what recent situations have you extended mercy? When have you consciously withheld mercy or, without meaning to, treated someone in a way that person considered harsh?

Rewriting the Beatitude

Write here your restatement of this week's beatitude and an opposite "Cursed are . . ." or "Woe to . . ." statement:

Positive: _____ are those who

_____

_____.

Negative:

_____

_____.

Notes for Group Session

My response to this week's beatitude will be

_____

_____.

To Will One Thing

Blessed are the pure in heart, for they will see God.
—Matthew 5:8

Of all the Beatitudes so far, this one seems to promise the greatest payoff. Imagine—to actually see God! For people who must "walk by faith, not by sight" (2 Cor. 5:7), to see God would be a blessing beyond anything we have known. But for most of us, this beatitude may also seem the least attainable. After all, when we think of purity of heart, we know ourselves to be less than pure, less than perfect in our thoughts, less than blameless in our actions. Even when we don't act on our jealousy, greed, desire to get even, or lust, we know that they're there. We're already doing the best we can and we're not pure in actions. So how can we ever hope to attain purity of heart? But such assumptions make purity of heart something different from its meaning in this passage. The word translated "pure" in this beatitude does not mean morally blameless and perfect. It means clear, as in understanding, or filled with one quality rather than a mixture of characteristics. The psalmist who wrote "O LORD, . . . give me an undivided heart to revere your name" (Ps. 86:11) was actually asking for what Jesus described. The psalmist asked for a heart set on honoring God, for what the Bible calls elsewhere "singleness of heart" (Eph. 6:5).

This psalmist was not alone in understanding that we need God's help to reach this state. The apostle Paul prayed for the Ephesians to have "the eyes of [their] heart enlightened" so they could know "the hope to which [God] has called" us (Eph. 1:18). This matter of willingness to allow our hearts to be changed lies at the center of seeking purity of heart. It involves willingness to let go of the multiple things that divide our heart and our attention so that we may do the "one thing [that] is needful" (Luke 10:42, KJV) for us. In another place, the apostle Paul wrote, "This one thing I do" (Phil. 3:13)—not "these many things I dabble in."

BECOMING A SCULPTOR

As these writers of scripture attest, we need help in seeing with an "undivided heart" how we are to live our faith. The good news is that Christ is willing to help us. As in the story of the healing of the blind man, even after meeting Christ and experiencing his touch, we may still see people "like trees, walking."(See Mark 8:22-26.) But just as Christ stayed with that man, touching him again until he could see clearly, we can trust Christ to stay with us and keep touching us. Christ will help us see clearly so we can come to a clear sense of God's purpose for us. This is an important step in our discipleship, because then our heart can be "single." As the Cheshire Cat said to Alice, if we don't care where we end up, any road will do. But once we understand what God has gifted and called us to do, we can avoid many of the side trails and detours that use our time and energy but do not move us toward what God asks. The old story about the sculptor applies here. As the sculptor works on a huge block of stone, a bystander asks, "What are you sculpting?"

"An elephant."

"That sounds very difficult. Is it?"

"Not at all. I just look at the stone and chip away everything that doesn't look like an elephant."

In a similar way, once we envision what God wants to make of our lives, we can begin to chip away what is not a part of that. We can begin to let go of baggage that weighs us down. We can begin to empty our hearts and our calendars so that we are less divided. This doesn't happen overnight; it is a process—and it has to be, because it involves changes that can take time.

I have felt for many years that God wanted me to spend more time writing. I realized my inner drive to write more than twenty years ago when someone asked me two simple questions: "What do you need in order to feel satisfied in a job? What do you have to be able to do to be happy?" I had not considered those questions before that moment. But as I replied, "I have to be able to teach, and I have to be able to write," my words settled into my heart as a revelation for me. I had known that I love teaching, and I have written since I was a child. But I had not articulated the truth that for me these two things are essentials. In that exchange, I learned something important about what God has placed within me.

Nevertheless, articulating that truth did not instantly change my life. Though I have kept a spiritual journal throughout my adult years, I never had much time left over for more substantial projects. I found ways do some writing around the edges of parenting and working. But this limited writing was not enough, and even though I knew that, my behavior did not change. When I write, I feel that I am fully alive, that I am doing what I was created to do. The process of writing exhilarates me. Many people are terrified by the mere prospect of facing a blank piece of paper, so I know that my feeling about writing is significant and that I should attend to this deep joy. Still, I was not writing beyond what was required in my work.

Then a series of events in my life made me face the fact that the years are passing quickly. If I was going to write as I said I need to do, I had to get started. But I couldn't realize my dream of writing because all my time was taken up by my life as I was living it. So I asked God to help me see where I could make changes that would give me time to write. The first changes were relatively easy and obvious: spend less time on the phone, less time watching television, less time cleaning house (proving that doing God's will is not always a painful sacrifice). I also realized that a shorter commute could give me an additional ninety minutes every day. I began planning to move closer to work, and when circumstances were right, I moved to a much smaller place—little more than half the size of what I left. This required me to give up much of the "stuff" I had accumulated over the years, which also freed the time I spent taking care of all the stuff. It freed additional time to read, to think, to pray—and to write. After the sense of urgency surfaced about paying attention to my dream, it took me almost four years to make the move that has made such a difference for me.

Perhaps you also have a dream that you have nurtured—maybe in secret. Take a moment to think about this: When do you feel most alive? What must you have in your life to be deeply satisfied? How can this joy be used for and by God?

The process of sorting continues in my life. Over the last three years, God has been nagging me about developing clearer priorities in my discipleship. God does not deal subtly with me (I think I'm too thickheaded for that to work well), and I found myself barraged with information about "personal mission statements." At first I discounted these as no more than a gimmick, like those used in positive-thinking seminars—"Write on a three-by-five card this affirmation about where you want to be five years from now, and repeat it to yourself every morning and evening until it becomes reality." But I couldn't get away from people talking about personal mission statements. I had to read a book in preparation for a seminar, and much of it centered on developing corporate and personal mission statements. I went to supervisor's training, and one of the first sessions involved writing a personal mission statement. One of the women in my new accountability group came into one of our first meetings talking about her personal mission statement. I reached the point that I almost wouldn't have been surprised if someone in the supermarket checkout line had turned to me and said, "So, do you have a personal mission statement? They're great. Mine has changed my life."

DEFINING A PATH

Once I decided to start paying attention, it seemed there were articles on personal mission in nearly every magazine or newspaper I picked up. Many good books are available on the subject. Stephen Covey's *First Things First* and *The 7 Habits of Highly Effective People* are well known. A specifically Christian treatment is Tom and Christine Sine's *Living on Purpose: Finding God's Best for Your Life*. Workshops on identifying spiritual gifts also prove helpful in clarifying a sense of purpose and defining a personal mission, because God's purpose for our life builds on our gifts. I took part in one of these to confirm what I had learned earlier about myself.

One structure that has helped me think about my personal mission comes from Rick Warren's book *The Purpose-Driven Life*. He uses the acronym SHAPE to describe the elements of personal mission:

Spiritual gifts

Heart

Abilities

Personality

Experiences[1]

The Bible gives us several lists of *spiritual gifts,* the first item in Warren's acronym: Ephesians 4:4-8, 11-13; 1 Corinthians 12:4-20, 28; and Romans 12:1-8. Discovering our personal gifts for expressing God's purposes in the world is a primary concern for believers. As the Bible tells us, the Holy Spirit gives God's people varied gifts but for one purpose: to build up the body of Christ and bring us to maturity. Identifying and honoring one another's gifts empowers us to use them more effectively, while also making us accountable to one another.

Heart, the second element of the acronym, has to do with identifying our passions—what we really care about, what excites us, what stirs our energies and elicits an inward response. Some people seem to think that answering God's call means turning their back on what they truly enjoy, but I believe God puts our passions within us to energize us and lead us toward what we are meant to do with our lives. Following God's will for us is not meant to be a grim enterprise in self-abnegation. Though the psalmist who wrote that God "will give you the desires of your heart" (37:4) probably did not mean that phrase as I apply it here, I have come to believe that the deep desires of our heart, the ones deep within us that stay year after year and do not go away, are put there by God. Our passions and desires are part of who God made us to be, and paying attention to them can help us discover and define our mission. As Proverbs 20:27 says, "The human spirit is the lamp of the Lord."

The third element, *abilities,* refers to inborn aptitudes and inclinations that we can work to develop. Some people are born seeming to understand and love numbers. Some are born with mechanical aptitude, some with musical ability, some with love for organization and order, some with the ability to learn many languages, some with a curiosity about and love for science, some with empathy for and ability to relate to all kinds of people, and so on. Each of us has a unique assortment of abilities and talents. Some are obvious from childhood, and some we discover later in life.

The fourth item in Warren's acronym is *personality.* I like the fact that he includes this as one of the elements in discovering our purpose because it often seems that tools for assessing our gifts ignore personality. Some of us are extroverts who process information and encounter the world through interacting with people and our environment. Some are introverts who prefer to process information in solitude, in reflection. While extroverts are energized by interacting with people, introverts are energized by solitude and silence. Some of us experience the world by handling and manipulating physical reality; some of us find the world within our minds at least as compelling as outer reality and love ideas, theories, planning, experimenting. These differences affect the way we use our abilities and spiritual gifts. An introvert with the spiritual gift of serving will probably exercise that gift in a different way than an extrovert with the gift of serving. Understanding and accepting differences in personality can free us to appreciate the different ways we approach tasks.

The final letter in the acronym, *E,* stands for *experience.* I had a friend who was a missionary pilot. His training in flying and experience with small planes (along with his spiritual gift of serving, his outgoing personality, and his mechanical aptitude) became part of fulfilling God's call in his life as he ferried medical personnel, supplies, and preachers all over West Africa. In a similar way, all our experiences and skills can help us discover our call. God, the ultimate economist and recycler, never lets anything go to waste. All the experiences of our lives—our wrenching losses, our dearest successes, and everything in between—shape us and become one of the resources God can use to extend Christ's healing ministry into our world.

Avoiding Detours

All that we understand about ourselves and about the will of God can help us reach clarity about how we are to spend our energy, in order to move toward having a heart filled with one purpose. We can never do everything that needs to be done. There are more good causes and more needy people than any one of us could ever respond to. But a clear sense of our personal mission allows us to see the world differently, to listen with a more discerning ear to the appeals that come to us, to make decisions more faithfully. My mission statement helps me decide whether a particular invitation fits with what I am to do with my life—or whether it is someone else's opportunity. Having a clear statement of purpose helps me "see God" in ordinary situations; that statement also challenges me to respond because it removes the "wiggle room" that allows me to rationalize not acting.

Let me give you an example of how a personal mission statement works. One of the women in my accountability group has a mission statement that begins, "To live a simplified lifestyle of daily attentiveness to God. . . ." A relative told her and her husband about a house that "would be just perfect for" them. Then a real estate agent in their church approached them about the same house. They decided that they ought to at least look, since they had been considering a different living situation. The house was beautiful, and it had several attractive features that did indeed seem perfect for them. They decided to think and pray about it. As they discussed all that would be involved in relocating and caring for the property, they came to see that buying this new house would complicate their lifestyle considerably. Since they were committed to a "simplified" lifestyle, they were able to say no to the possibility with confidence that their decision was right. (Time has shown them that it was.)

A good mission statement shines light on our daily life and choices. It must be specific enough to give direction not only about what to say yes to but also about what to say no to—as it did my friends about buying a house. A general statement such as "To be a faithful disciple of Jesus Christ" doesn't meet the test of being personal because it applies to all believers. A good personal mission statement draws together the ministry gifts God has given us, the deep affections of our heart, and the needs of the world. In the book *Wishful Thinking: A Theological ABC,* Frederick Buechner defines *vocation* as the place "where your deep gladness and the world's deep hunger meet."[2] Your "deep gladness" is what stirs your heart, gives you energy, and makes you feel most fully alive.

FINDING HELP IN SCRIPTURE

Study of scripture helps us to define our personal mission. If we place ourselves in a listening posture with the question of purpose in mind, God will speak. The lists of spiritual gifts help us think about the different roles we might have in serving God. Another verse I find helpful in exploring personal call is Isaiah 50:4: "The LORD God has given me the tongue of a teacher, that I may know how to sustain the weary with a word." In working with writers, I use a paraphrase of that verse, "The Lord God has given me the pen of a writer, that I may . . ." and have them complete the sentence to explore what they want to write. The verse can prove useful in beginning to define our mission if we change a few words. For instance, "The Lord God has given me the heart of a nurturer, that I may _____" or, "The Lord God has given me the hands of a _____" or, "the mind of a _____, that I may _____." Essentially, this verse can help us to think about what is central to our identity and to explore ways God can use that central value.

We can also sharpen our focus using the same verse to consider the group or area God calls us to. Isaiah was to help "the weary." What people or cause do you care deeply about? Children? The elderly? What group of people consistently tugs at your heart? To whom are you drawn? Answering those questions can help you discern where God is leading you.

Tom and Christine Sine, whose book I mentioned previously, draw their personal mission statement from Proverbs 31:8-9: "Speak out for those who cannot speak, for the rights of all the destitute. Speak out, judge righteously, defend the rights of the poor and needy." Their mission is "to become a voice for those who have no voice and bring glimpses of God's shalom kingdom into people's lives."[3] Christine has worked with Mercy Ships among the poor in Asia, Africa, and Latin America, and Tom has worked with World Concern in Haiti. Their mission grows out of the deep affections of their hearts, building on a passage of scripture that captures their passion and places it within the scope of what God wants, not just for them but for the larger world.

Why do I think that personal mission statements have anything to do with the beatitude "Blessed are the pure in heart"? Because I agree with Søren Kierkegaard's statement, "Purity of heart is to will one thing." As we discern and state the "one thing" for which God means us to use our time, energy, and other resources, our vision of the world changes. Instead of seeing an overwhelming array of needs that we could never address, we begin to see specific places where God's light is needed and where our skills and gifts can make a difference. We begin to see the face of Christ in the needy faces around us. Once we gain clarity about our own gifts and calling, we also realize that we can no longer get away with saying all the time, "That is someone else's opportunity."

LEARNING TO SAY NO

When we set our hearts on being faithful to the "one thing" for which God has gifted and called us, the clutter that can sometimes block our view disappears. We can see which tasks and involvements are consistent with our primary gifts and values and which ones need to fall away in order to free time and energy for what matters most: doing God's will. Does this mean we no longer consider any of the requests close at hand? Of course not. Sometimes organizing the closet or cleaning the garage is important to our personal mission if someone we love feels it must be done. Time spent in some tasks is primarily an investment in relationship; this can incarnate our love for and commitment to another person. But in every arena, as we define what is ours to do, we also increase our ability to see what is *not* ours to do. Then when we are asked to do something—even something worthwhile—that is not a part of our mission, we can say no. In fact, we should say no in order that the person whose mission it is meant to be will eventually be asked. If we do not learn to say no, good people will take up all our time and energy with good things they want us to do. We must learn to say no to people in order to remain free to say yes to God.

How do we do this? One of my coworkers modeled for me the attitude and words that helped me formulate my standard "no" response. I had asked her to serve on a committee, and she phoned to respond. She said, "Thank you so much for asking me to do this. It sounds like a great opportunity, and it's a compliment that you think I can contribute. But I have to say no. Thanks again." I was impressed by her graciousness and her finality, and I determined to remember what she had said and how she said it. Later, when one of my pastors asked me to serve in an area of our church that does not fit with my gifts and passion, I said, "Thanks so much for asking me. This is a worthwhile ministry, and it's a compliment that you think I can do this. But I have to say no to this in order to say yes to God's primary call in my life." What can even the pastor say in response to that? (I also committed to pray for him to find the people whose calling and gifts fit the task that needed to be done.)

I am not saying that our lives and all our choices become easy once we identify our gifts and define the arena where we can most joyfully (remember "your deep gladness"?) serve God. We still will face conflicts of good with good, when competing demands pull at us. And though our gifts remain constant, our specific acts of faithfulness vary as time passes and our circumstances change. But on any given day, we commit as much of ourselves as we understand to as much of God as we understand. We dedicate ourselves to an open-ended relationship with God, using our gifts and skills for God's purposes. And Jesus promised that if we remain clearly committed to that, we will see God.

DAILY REFLECTIONS FOR WEEK 6

Day 1—Read Matthew 13:44-46.

What is the "treasure" or the two or three most important "pearls" you seek in life? What are you willing to sacrifice for?

Each day we give that day of our lives in exchange for something. What did you trade the last twenty-four hours of your life for? Do you consider this a worthwhile trade?

How does seeking the "pearls" that you value shape your choices about how you spend your time, money, and energy?

List three or four primary relationships in your life. What attention have you given each of these in the last week? in the last month? How well does your recent behavior reflect how much you say you value these relationships?

Day 2—Read Mark 10:46-52.

Imagine that you are the blind man in this story and that Jesus has come to you. Listen as Jesus says, "What do you want me to do for you?" How would you answer?

What voices tell you to be quiet, as the people in the crowd did the blind man, and hold you back from seeking what you truly want? Who or what holds you back from getting what you need?

Where do you limit what you ask of God? Are there some requests you will not make of God? Why or why not?

What do you value most in life? What do you want to ask of God regarding this?

Day 3—Read Isaiah 50:4.

The servant in Isaiah says that God has made him a teacher. If you were writing a sentence like this one to describe yourself, what two or three roles would you name as primary for your life? (Some suggestions: builder, nurturer, healer, leader, speaker, writer, helper, organizer, guide, encourager.)

If you were writing a sentence like this one to describe yourself, what ability/quality would you name in place of *tongue*? (Suggestions: skills, mind, heart, hands, compassion, education, personality, experience.)

The servant in Isaiah says God has given him this role and skills so that he will know how to "sustain." For what purpose has God given you abilities, skills, passions, and personality? (Suggestions: help, guide, teach, comfort, lead, sustain, defend, heal, speak for.)

Verse 4 names a group to whom God has sent the servant: the weary. What particular group of people or area of ministry touches you deeply, that you seem to "always" have cared about? (Suggestions: the weary, the defenseless, the sick, the hungry or homeless, the unchristian, children, youth, the elderly, people "like you"—your class, ethnic group, personality.)

Combine your answers to these questions to write a description of yourself using the pattern of Isaiah 50:4:

The Lord God has given me _____ of a

_____, that I might _____ the

_____.

Day 4—Read 1 Corinthians 12:1-12 and Ephesians 4:7-16.

According to 1 Corinthians 12, what is the result of our using the gifts God gives us?

According to Ephesians 4:7, for what purpose are gifts given to believers? What must each of us do to see that this purpose is fulfilled?

Looking back on yourself five years ago, in what ways have you matured in your faith? In what ways are you clearer now about serving God than you used to be?

These passages make clear that not all members of the body of Christ have the same function. What gifts do you see in others that you wish you had? Why are these gifts attractive to you?

Day 5—Take a spiritual gifts inventory.

Complete the spiritual gifts inventory given to you by the session leader at your last meeting (available at www.equippedforeverygoodwork.org). Score it by adding your responses across each row of the response sheet.

For which two gifts did you have the highest scores?

What are your two next strongest gifts? How have you used these in serving God and others in the past week?

Rewriting the Beatitude

Write here your restatement of this week's beatitude and an opposite "Cursed are . . ." or "Woe to . . . " statement.

Positive: _____ are those who

_____

_____.

Negative:

_____

_____.

Notes for Group Session

My response to this week's beatitude will be

_____

_____.

Seeing the World
Needy and Whole

**Blessed are the peacemakers, for they will be called
the children of God.**

—Matthew 5:9

"Wa r! . . . . What is it good for? Absolutely . . . nothing" goes a song that was popular during my teen years. I grew up during a tumultuous time; my generation was shaped by division about U.S. involvement in Vietnam. Several of my high-school classmates died there. We thought no one else could understand the pain of our experience. But my father was wounded in World War II, and his friends were killed. In my grand-mother's time, thousands died in World War I, the "war to end all wars." My great-grandfather's contemporaries died in the Spanish-American war. In my great-great-grandmother's time, friends and husbands and brothers died in the Civil War. In her parents' time it was the War of 1812, and before that, the Revolutionary War. The picture dismays: rarely has more than thirty years elapsed between times of armed conflict. Every U.S. generation for more than 200 years has seen war claim the lives of its people. Peace seems elusive, at the very least. Yet as Jesus' words in this beatitude tell us, peace is something close to God's heart. In fact, those who work for peace are claimed as God's sons and daughters.

The people to whom Jesus spoke this beatitude lived in an occupied country—a country with an uneasy peace. Imperial Rome's soldiers were everywhere, directing the daily lives of Jesus' listeners. (One of them, a centurion, figures in a Gospel story about Jesus healing someone long-distance.) The Romans were not loving and gentle taskmasters. They forced the Jews around them to carry loads for them; they controlled the economy, exacting taxes and arresting those who refused to pay; and they ran the legal system. Romans were not well-loved, and they were every-where. In this setting, Jesus had the courage to talk about peacemakers and to say that they are the ones who will be called "children of God."

The Jews viewed the label "children of God" as their title, both their destiny and a promise that God would surely fulfill. Deuteronomy 14:12 says, "You are children of the LORD your God. . . . You are a people holy to the LORD your God; it is you the LORD has chosen out of all the peoples on earth to be his people, his treasured possession." The prophet Hosea said, "The number of the people of Israel shall be like the sand of the sea, which can be neither measured nor numbered; and in the place where it was said to them, 'You are not my people,' it shall be said to them, 'Chil-dren of the living God'" (Hos. 1:10). In a way, Jesus was saying that his hearers could claim their destiny and confirm their identity by working for peace. And for the first three hundred years of Christianity's history, Christians refused to take up arms, showing that they understood peace-making to be central to their role in the world. Pacifism was, in fact, a pri-mary trait that distinguished Christians from the culture around them. (This refusal to take up arms to defend themselves was what part of made believers a spectacle in the Roman arenas.) They believed that God did not want them to take part in war or violence, and many who work to end wars in the world still do so because of their faith in Christ.

NEITHER WAR NOR PEACE

The peace that Christ came to bring is more than just the absence of war. Certainly Jesus' hearers knew that. They lived in a situation that clarified this difference. They were not actively at war, but neither did they live in peace. The lives of the Jews were limited by this political reality. But they were also limited by illness and by estrangement from God and one another. They were looking for a political messiah, someone who would come and restore them as a power among the nations; but Jesus came to bring a more personal and yet simultaneously more far-reaching peace.

In the Hebrew scripture that Jesus knew and quoted, the word usually translated "peace" is *shalom.* This word means much more than not being at war. It can also be translated "salvation" or "wholeness." This kind of peace is bringing salvation to—mending and making whole—the entire created order, in the sense that God brings healing from all that limits us. In Luke 4:18, Jesus claims this as his mission: "To bring good news to the poor . . . to proclaim release to the captives and recovery of sight to the blind, to let the oppressed go free." Peacemakers are all those who work to end conditions that constrict others' lives. Jesus said that he came to give us "life . . . to the full" (John 10:10, NIV)— "life . . . more abundantly," as the King James Version puts it. Anything that keeps people from the fullness of life that Jesus offered is antiwholeness, antishalom. Christ wants to free us from all that limits the life of God in us and around us.

In his book *The Kingdom Within,* John Sanford explains that this deep and far-reaching wholeness is the essence of the new kingdom Christ came to bring. This is why Jesus regarded sickness as a kind of alienation from God and why the new kingdom and healing go together.[1] Wherever antiwholeness exists, God's kingdom opposes it, and so Jesus goes through the towns and villages, "proclaiming the good news of the kingdom and curing every disease and every sickness among the people" (Matt. 4:23; 9:35). This new kingdom was carried forward by Peter and John in the proclamation and healings recorded in the book of Acts, and this was to be the nature of the work of those who followed Christ. As John's Gospel promises, those who believe in Christ "will do greater works than these" (14:1). Sanford says that when the kingdom of God is being established in an individual, that person is becoming whole.[2] And I would add, as we move toward wholeness, we come to want the same for others. Once we catch a vision of what God wants for people and for the world, we become willing to rearrange our lives. Our priorities change, so that we are willing to set our minds first on this kingdom, to seek the righteousness—the rightness and wholeness—of the world as it can be when fully reconciled to God.

This is the sense of salvation contained in the shalom vision, when we and our world are redeemed—bought back—from the evil that seeks to destroy wholeness. We are released from the hold of sin as we live in what Rosemary Radford Ruether calls "healing union with God,"[3] which then issues in compassion for others. We become servants for others, seeking to help them experience the connection with God that heals us and can heal them as well. As 2 Corinthians 5:17-19 puts it, in Christ we are "a new creation" and God has given us a role in "reconciling the world to himself, . . . entrusting the message of reconciliation to us."

TOO MUCH TO DO

This charge from God brings us again to acknowledge our poverty. In the face of the world's great needs, anything that one of us might do could be only a puny response. It helps to remember that Jesus said peacemakers will be called not "mighty men" of God, as David's soldiers were described in Hebrew scripture, but "children of God." We are to be children in the best sense of the word—full of hope, ready to love, generous, knowing we are dependent on our Parent, learning from and imitating God, going to God for reassurance and courage when we face the world's needs and see the poverty of our resources to meet them. We are also like children in the sense that God takes a risk in entrusting this work to us, just as we take a risk when we become parents, for our children can choose a way that we know leads away from life. Rubem Alves calls us a "divine adventure," for God knows that we are "capable of planting gardens and of building concentration camps, capable of choosing life or of choosing death."[4]

And as history shows us, we have done both. That is the reason the world so badly needs to hear the message of wholeness, of shalom, of the peace God wants for all of us. The dehumanizing systems that oppress God's children around the world are created by people like us. Injustice, violence, economic and sexual exploitation, slavery in all its forms, and all the small and comfortable evils that we see every day spring from our human failings. They grow from our lust for power over others and from our greed. Shalom does not envision escape from the world but engagement with the world in all its brokenness, so that "justice [can] roll down like waters and righteousness like an ever-flowing stream" (Amos 5:24). Peacemakers are those who see that the world and its people are broken but also hold a dream, a vision, that God can and does reach out to heal our world. And God does it through the acts of those who live by the values of this new kingdom where God's will is being done.

Working for peace means challenging the powers that oppress people. Evils abound—prostitution; child labor and slave labor; the child sex trade; the drug culture that enslaves so many; corporate greed, theft, irresponsibility, and deception ("cooking the books," looting pension plans). Lack also oppresses many. Starvation and malnutrition continue, even though the planet produces enough food to feed everyone. Millions suffer because of inadequate health care, homelessness, no access to education. All of these situations are entangled with systems that are complex and difficult to change. But someone must challenge them, and the scriptures tell us this also is part of God's work. When Mary and Joseph took the infant Jesus into the Temple, Simeon told them that this child would "be for the falling and the rising of many in Israel" (Luke 2:34); Mary's song while visiting Elizabeth declared trust in God who brings "down the powerful from their thrones" and lifts up "the lowly," who scatters the proud, who fills "the hungry with good things" and "sends the rich away empty." (See Luke 1:46-55.)

Peacemaking often involves dismantling entrenched power. We see this when we consider Gandhi's efforts to do away with the oppression of the caste system or Martin Luther King Jr. working to end segregation and ensure civil rights or the Sisters of Loretto working for justice for coal miners in West Virginia. This is the work of a God who changes the usual order of things, who rocks the boat, who deposes those in high positions. And this is the God we serve.

As we respond to the world's needs, God does not call all of us to confront the same problems or powers that stand in the way of wholeness, nor to confront them in the same ways. Each of us with our unique constellation of spiritual gifts, abilities, passions, and experiences responds uniquely. This is why a clear sense of our individual call from God is so important. So much needs to be done that we could be immobilized by the enormity of the challenges if we felt that we had to do it all. But we do not have to be involved on all the fronts where change is needed. None of us is meant to assume responsibility for all of the world. God's call is much simpler and much closer than that: God calls each of us to act for justice and wholeness *within our sphere of influence.*

TINY TRANSFORMATIONS

That may seem a small response, but each response has the power to change a part of the world. I heard a news report about a program to teach preschoolers nonviolent ways of resolving disputes, in contrast to the competitive models shown in action movies and cartoons. Teachers and aides who work with these children have no illusions that they will transform the entire culture, but they can teach these children a better way. Touching a single life can change many lives.

After the killings and suicides at Columbine High School several years ago, I found myself thinking about the two young shooters. Could they have been different, their lives and actions been different, if years earlier some Christian teacher or neighbor or scout leader had been a peacemaker by trying to bring wholeness in those boys' lives? Could someone have invested time in them and turned their lives in a different direction? Surely some of God's people had contact with these boys. Surely they encountered Christians somewhere along the way to growing up. If someone had been sensitive to the Spirit's nudgings and noticed a troubled child, maybe life could have been different for one of those boys—and therefore for the other one and for all those whose lives were affected by their actions. I don't mean to imply that no one tried to reach them; perhaps many people did. Such acts would not have seemed spectacular, of course—just ordinary kindnesses. But those who acted would have been peacemakers in the truest sense of bringing shalom.

In other unspectacular ways, we have opportunities to make peace. I think of my former neighbor, George (not his real name). Our condo association was embroiled in a fight (homeowner associations often seem to be, for some reason), and this one had become particularly nasty. Talk of lawsuits filled neighborhood conversations. After our second or third called meeting, we seemed to be getting nowhere. George, a quiet man, rarely says more than a pleasant hello. But after this meeting, he took time to write a letter to all of us, encouraging us to approach the situation with fairness and respect for one another. He urged us to remain calm and to consider carefully how we could resolve the dispute without further damaging relationships. In that unspectacular act, George was being a peacemaker. Such actions don't get mentioned in the newspaper, but they remind us that making peace does not have to be spectacular to be genuine and effective.

Reconciliation and redemption are needed in myriad places, with many groups. A program in my city works to help women caught in the snare of prostitution. There are hundreds if not thousands of prostitutes in our metropolitan area, and this program helps only a few—but it does try to help those few. Our city offers sports programs to help inner-city kids avoid gang involvement, programs to help abused children and women, discussion groups to foster understanding between diverse citizens, recycling groups, tutoring programs to help kids having trouble in school, groups working to make government more responsive to needs of low-income citizens, groups working to reform the education system, music programs for kids living in subsidized housing, drug and alcohol rehab programs, groups working with jail and prison inmates to help them learn to read or to be better parents—the list of worthwhile efforts seems endless. All of these people work to bring wholeness, to bring peace in the deep and lasting sense of helping people learn to live together in justice and respect; they are peacemakers.

A FAMILY RESEMBLANCE

I began by reminding us that being called "children of God" is part of God's promise. This beatitude challenges us to ask ourselves what we want to be "called" by our life. Even more important, what "family resemblance" do people see between us and God? How have we acted to bring reconciliation? What time, risk, effort, or sacrifice does God ask of us? This beatitude offers us a lasting identity in connection with God. But this identity depends on our claiming the role of one who brings healing.

In the Orthodox tradition, Mary the mother of Jesus is known as *theoto-kos*—literally, "God-bearer." When we work for peace and reconciliation with God, we also are God-bearers; we bring God into the lives of those who may not have understood that God wants fullness of life for them.

Jesus used the plural here—*peacemakers*—implying that this is not a task for any one of us alone and that the world needs more than one kind of peacemaker. So we explore the different aspects of peacemaking and the different contexts in which each of us is called to act for peace. At home, at work, in the church, the community, the world—we are different, and our role in peacemaking varies in all these places. We use different skills.

Peacemaking is active. It is not enough to pray for peace or to try to live peaceably. We must also work for justice, investing ourselves in our communities for the good of all. Even though we are not permanent residents of this world, we have a role to play while we are here. God's plan is not pie in the sky, on high, by and by when we die. We are meant to make a difference here and now.

The prophet Jeremiah wrote to God's people in exile, giving them a plan for action while living in a culture that did not accept their values. He told them, "Build houses and live in them; plant gardens and eat what they produce. Take wives and have sons and daughters. . . . Seek the welfare [shalom] of the city where I have sent you into exile, and pray to the LORD on its behalf, for in its welfare [shalom] you will find your welfare" [shalom] (Jer. 29:5-7). This is still good advice to us in our "exile," living in a culture that does not operate by kingdom values. We are to "build houses"—to provide for immediate needs. We are to "plant"—to invest in efforts that will bear fruit in the future. And we are to pray and act for the welfare of our "city," for our wholeness depends in part on its wholeness.

Where do you hear our needy world calling for someone to come and help? Where can you see a situation that needs changing? What do you believe God wants for the world?

Peacemakers are those who, seeing the world's needs, also hold in their hearts a vision of the world made whole. When we act to make that vision a reality, we claim our identity as God's sons and daughters.

DAILY REFLECTIONS FOR WEEK 7

Day 1—Read Luke 4:16-18.

In this passage Jesus describes the groups of people God has sent him to help. Who would these be in your community?

Which of these groups have you had contact with? To which of them does your church reach out in its ministry?

Who are the oppressed in our world? Who oppresses them, and for what reasons or results?

How has God "anointed" you to reach out to one of these groups? What group are you drawn to, and what experience causes you to care about them?

Day 2—Read Matthew 10:34-39 and 16:24-26.

When have you seen situations where someone's faith caused division?

What does this passage say to you about opposition to doing what God wants?

Jesus was a healer, yet he was continually opposed. When does doing good lead to opposition in our culture?

What do you feel when you read Jesus' words about denying self and taking up the cross? Have you ever felt you were doing that? If so, what was the situation? If not, have you ever done something difficult because you felt your faith required it?

How could losing our life ever help us to find it? What sense do you make of this advice for ordinary people?

Day 3—Read Matthew 25:31-46.
Which categories of people named in this passage have you helped? What ministries to these groups is your congregation involved in? Which ones have you participated in, or if you have not, which are you drawn to?

Where have you recently encountered a person in need of the basics of life, and how did you respond?

Have you ever done something for someone and felt that you were doing it for Christ? If so, what helped you to serve with this awareness? If not, how could you help yourself remember to look for Christ in the next needy person you meet?

Day 4—Read 2 Corinthians 3:2-6.

What "letter" do you want to write with your life? What do you want to leave as your legacy?

How do you think those in your family, church, workplace, and neighborhood would describe your values, based on your actions? What would cause them to describe you as Christian?

How has God's message been "written on" your heart? Who has taught you about the faith and modeled it for you?

Verse 6 says, "The letter kills, but the Spirit gives life." How have you seen rules used to kill the human spirit? In contrast, how and where have you seen grace give life?

Day 5—Read John 10:7-11 and 14:12.

Considering what Jesus did for people, what would you say was his definition of having "life . . . abundantly"?

What is your community of faith doing to continue Christ's work for peace in its broadest sense of wholeness and unity? Where are you working to change conditions, laws, and institutions that keep people from experiencing fullness of life?

Rewriting the Beatitude

Write here your restatement of this week's beatitude and an opposite "Cursed are . . ." or "Woe to . . ." statement:

Positive: _____ are those who

_____

_____.

Negative:

_____

_____.

Notes for Group Session

My response to this week's beatitude will be

_____

_____.

Action and Reaction

**Blessed are those who are persecuted for righteousness' sake,
for theirs is the kingdom of heaven.**

—Matthew 5:10

After this eighth beatitude, Jesus goes on to say, "Blessed are you when people revile you and persecute you and utter all kinds of evil against you falsely on my account. Rejoice and be glad, for your reward is great in heaven, for in the same way they persecuted the prophets who were before you." These words aren't fun to hear. In fact, for privileged Christians like us, they may be even more difficult to hear than the beatitudes about being meek and poor in spirit.

The gospel of prosperity has so permeated Western culture that we somewhat resemble the Jews I mentioned in chapter 1: we see our blessings as proof of God's favor. Some people even say they are our "right" as the children of a generous God. We live in a country where, for the most part, we do not suffer persecution for being Christian. On the contrary, people of other faiths claim that in the United States, Christians enjoy positive bias, while those of other faiths experience discrimination in jobs, housing, and the legal system. Being a Christian here does not automatically bring persecution, as it does for believers in many places.

In fact, we feel almost entitled to a good life. Martin Luther King Jr. once said in a sermon that we have rewritten the Great Commission to say, "Go ye into all the world, keep your blood pressure down, and lo, I will make you a well-adjusted personality."[1] In other words, we expect that following Christ will bring us perks. We expect that, for the most part, if we live in relationship with God and try to do what is right, life will mostly be okay. The continuing popularity of Harold S. Kushner's book *When Bad Things Happen to Good People* implies that we have trouble accepting the reality that book addresses, as if we think bad things shouldn't happen to good people—people like us.

Most of us are not so crass as to say we expect God to make us rich, but we do often seem to expect that we will at least have stable, happy families, peace of mind, good health care if not good health, and various psychological advantages because of our faith. We assume that if we are honest and hardworking, we will always be able to find and keep a good job. We cannot conceive of situations like those faced by Christians in India, for example, where government jobs and advancement in almost all jobs outside the church depend on caste and connections. Christians may be actively excluded from the inner circles of decision making in businesses and social institutions. For most of us, being Christian carries no physical, social, or career risk, and we are probably glad to be able to say that we have never felt persecuted for our faith.

LIVING THE GOOD LIFE

This is not true for believers in many countries. Recently a missions group from my church went to Russia to visit and work with our sister congregation in Perovo. One of our pastors went along, and she told us about an incident that changed her perceptions of what it means to publicly live the faith. The group from Perovo and the group from our church had been working together, and before parting for the day they joined hands to pray. They were standing quietly outside in front of the church building they had been working on. People living in nearby apartments leaned out their windows to see what was going on, and soon a police car arrived. The police officer asked what the group was doing, as if this were an unlawful assembly (as it would have been under Communist rule). Someone living nearby had called the police. After a tense exchange with the church members, the officer got in his patrol car to leave. Then he deliberately backed the car into the group. They had to scatter to avoid being hit. Our pastor said, "And these people endure such attention whenever they publicly profess faith." Even when they are not doing anything wrong, those around them mistrust their motives and call the police. Even the police try to make life difficult for them. Most of us cannot imagine such a situation, and we certainly don't want to see it repeated in any version in our lives. After all, who wants to endure pain and hostility? The natural inclination is to avoid pain.

However, Jesus says in this passage that not only can we find blessing in persecution, but also we should rejoice when it comes! (This is the only beatitude that includes an imperative—"Rejoice.") Perhaps we can come closer to matching the incredulity of Jesus' original hearers here than with any of these sayings. This beatitude makes no sense. Let's face it—we are not "into" suffering. Just as we shy away from mourning our losses, we shy away from words about the difficulties of discipleship. We don't want it to be tough. We don't want to do without, to extend ourselves, to die to self. It's just not the American way.

Italian journalist Beppe Severgnini wrote a book about our national identity and obsessions titled *Ciao, America!: An Italian Discovers the U.S.* He lived for a year in Georgetown, a section of Washington, D.C., to immerse himself in our culture and observe our national character. According to Severgnini, Americans are obsessed with three things: comfort, control, and competition. He sees expected conveniences like air-conditioning and central heating as metaphors for our "right" to be comfortable all the time and to demonstrate our control of the uncontrollable—the effects of weather, specifically, and by extension, the world at large. Competition permeates business as well as sports (witness the Fortune 500 lists of richest people, highest-grossing businesses, and highest-paid executives), and those who finish in second place are losers in every field. I thought of this during the last winter Olympic Games when various silver medalists talked about not realizing their dreams and trying again in four years. Why is finishing second in the world a bad result? Because it's not first, and we expect and want to be first. Anything less is not really winning. As unflattering as Severgnini's observations may seem, I think they are accurate. We are in many ways the world's most arrogant 800-pound gorilla. And nobody, but nobody, pushes us around and gets away with it.

So, Jesus said, when people tell lies about us and push us around because we pursue righteousness, we're supposed to feel good about that? And we're supposed to be glad because someday, in heaven, we will be rewarded? Most of us can't delay gratification for a few hours (think about the chocolate candy or cookies calling to us from the kitchen while we watch TV in the evening), and Jesus said we have to wait until we get to heaven? This beatitude makes outrageous claims.

POWER PUSHES BACK

The beatitude also takes us back to where we started. (The first and eighth beatitudes both end with "for theirs is the kingdom of heaven"—another set of bookends.) Jesus began this discourse by saying that those who are poor in spirit—those who depend entirely on God for everything—own the kingdom of God. How can the poor own it all? That first beatitude turned the usual order on its ear, and here Jesus does it again. Those who make righteousness their agenda, who seek to reconcile the world to God, will encounter resistance and should rejoice when it happens. That doesn't make sense. Or does it? I recall something I heard a politician say recently. In our state, we're involved in a fight about tax reform, and various plans have been suggested. A reporter interviewed a legislator who said, "If people on both ends of the spectrum are upset, we must be doing something right." That person knew change always elicits opposition. People squeal when their vested interests are threatened.

Entrenched power hates challenges that threaten its control—and usually its money. The business section of our local newspaper recently carried a headline that said, "Watchdog groups castigate [a drug company]." The article concerned a lawsuit filed because a whistle-blower, an insider, had alleged illegal activities by the company. Further on in the same section, another headline said the same drug company "sues whistle-blower, subpoenas woman's attorney." When we push against wrong, it pushes back. If we work to make our communities more like God wants them to be, more loving and just, then we should expect opposition. Whether "the mighty" we depose from their thrones are our personal idols, tyrannies, and spoiled behaviors or the "principalities" and "powers" (Eph. 6:12, KJV) against which we struggle on a larger scale, these will resist giving up their place on the throne. In fact, if there is no struggle, we should ask ourselves why not. When we attempt to displace entrenched evil, it digs in deeper and pushes against us. If we upset no one and experience no resistance, we may be busying ourselves with superficial issues and avoiding real ones.

When we try to turn ourselves and the world away from sin and self-centeredness and toward God, persecution will follow. All the thoughts and institutions that exalt themselves in opposition to Christ's ways will kick and scream and resist giving up their hold on us and on the power they have in the world. Tepid Christianity arouses no one's ire or resistance, but the cry for moderation ("Let's not go overboard here") is not a biblical ideal. Jesus said, "Sell your possessions, and give the money to the poor," not "Sell what you don't really need or use much." Jesus said, "Whoever loves father or mother . . . son or daughter more than me is not worthy of me," and, "Let the dead bury their own dead" (Matt. 19:21; 10:37; 8:22). The Bible asks us to give all we have, in full measure, realizing that persecution will follow. Just as Herod resisted the threat to his throne that he saw in the child Jesus and lashed out at all Jewish boys, worldly powers threatened with change lash out. Those who try to clean up their neighborhoods and get rid of crack houses find themselves threatened by drug merchants and their customers; those who work to defend the rights of the poor are harassed, and so on.

TRAINING FOR THE NEW WORLD

With this beatitude and in other places, Jesus was preparing his followers for what was to come, trying to help them understand that they would face difficult times, as he would. Like us, though, they did not want to hear these hard sayings. When Jesus tried to tell the disciples about the resistance he would face, about his coming suffering and death, Peter "took him aside and began to rebuke him, saying, 'God forbid it, Lord! This must never happen to you'" (Matt. 16:22). It is human nature to want not to hear such things.

But this beatitude reminds us to refocus our hope away from the temporary—our physical bodies and their ease or lack of it when persecution comes—and on what is eternal: our union with God. Living by this inner value, taking seriously the call to live God's new kingdom into existence, allows us to find joy in the midst of our struggles. It opens us up to heaven now, in the midst of this life. Because we are human creatures, tied to the earth, we constantly forget that this life is not all there is. As Paul told the Corinthians, our "momentary affliction" is part of God's working in us "an eternal weight of glory beyond all measure" for those who allow the process of refining us and redefining our priorities to go forward (2 Cor. 4:17). We can cooperate with God's purposes, or we can choose to avoid the narrow way of discipleship. John Sanford says that the process of entering God's kingdom is a process of becoming an individual. It requires stepping apart from the crowd, from the mass movements that are always the easier way, to suffer "the pain and difficulty of becoming a conscious person."[2] Paul's epistle to the Romans says we are "heirs of God and joint heirs with Christ—if, in fact, we suffer with him" (Rom. 8:17). That is, as the saying goes, a mighty big *if*.

This beatitude invites us to be one of the select few, to go through a process of allowing ourselves to be changed to identify with God's will and purposes on earth so that we become fit for the kingdom of God that is to come. We claim our role as God's children on earth by becoming peacemakers—those who set out to reconcile the world to God. As we act to bring healing to the world, the suffering that follows trains us to assume our eternal, lasting identity in the new kingdom. This is not a call to masochistic suffering for the sake of suffering, as in the sense "she has enjoyed ill health for years." It is not a call to a martyr complex. It isn't an assertion that suffering is always redemptive, though some suffering can be. This beatitude says clearly that when we suffer for the cause of righteousness—to put the world right with God—that suffering prepares us for the new kingdom. First Peter tells us that when we endure this "fiery ordeal," we rejoice because we are sharing Christ's sufferings (1 Pet. 4:12-13). Paul said, "I want to know Christ and the power of his resurrection and the sharing of his sufferings by becoming like him in his death" (Phil. 3:10), implying that we experience the power of the resurrection when we suffer for Christ.

Most of us are not called to die a literal, physical death as a part of following Christ, but we are called to die to self. This death moves us from being what Kierkegaard calls being an admirer of Jesus to being a true follower: "The admirer never makes any true sacrifices. He always plays it safe. . . . he renounces nothing, gives up nothing. . . . Not so for the follower. . . . The follower aspires with all his strength, with all his will to be what he admires. . . . And because of the follower's life, it will become evident who the admirers are, for the admirers will become agitated with him."[3]

Dying to our will and our desire for ease is part of the journey. Every day, we have opportunities to choose to please ourselves or to choose the more difficult, unpopular, new-kingdom way of trying to make the kingdoms of this world into the kingdoms of our God. Our acts may not be spectacular. We may do something as commonplace and uncomfortable as confronting a coworker who's telling racist jokes or speaking out in a community meeting about the need for more activities for teenagers. We may work for civil and human rights or for a more just tax code in our hometown or home state. Or we may go as missionaries to Afghanistan and be imprisoned by the Taliban, as two young American women were in 2001. Whatever our individual actions for Christ that arouse the wrath of the kingdoms of this world, this beatitude promises an eternal result.

A WINSOME MYSTERY

The church has always grown during times of persecution. In the first few centuries of the church's history, underground cells flourished. The catacombs of Rome testify to the devotion of the early believers and the danger they endured. Today the church continues to grow in China and in the former republics of the Soviet Union, even though the governments of those countries officially oppose it. As the church reemerges in Eastern bloc countries in Europe, we see that belief was not destroyed but actually strengthened under Communism. Perhaps persecution helps the church see more clearly what decisions need to be made, what actions must be taken. Perhaps persecution proves the truth of Christ's claims. Only people who have been genuinely changed from within will risk their ease and their lives. Those who see the courageous acts of believers are won to Christ because they see in us a life worth living. They see love that outlasts what the world dishes out.

In all the states acclaimed in these Beatitudes, Jesus sees a deeper reality than human reasoning can explain. Whether or not it is apparent to others, Jesus sees the playing out of these scenarios. He sees the ultimate outcome of being meek, of hungering for God, of acting for peace, of suffering to put the world right with God.

Exactly how our suffering joins us to Christ is a mystery that none of us will solve, and somehow I think the process is unique for each of us. But I do believe that continually refocusing our hearts, minds, and wills on God's kingdom allows us not to be captive to the pain and suffering that this world inevitably inflicts on those who confront its idolatries. Johannes Metz wrote that Christ, "with the full weight of his divinity . . . descended into the abyss of human existence. . . . He was not spared from the dark mystery of our poverty as human beings."[4] But Christ transformed that pain and poverty and made them a doorway into a new world by giving himself to what God wanted. We can choose to follow him through that door or to settle back into the easy chair of undemanding discipleship.

Paul's epistle to the Colossians urges us, "Seek the things that are above, where Christ is, seated at the right hand of God. Set your minds on things that are above, not on things that are on earth" (3:1-2). When we care more about doing things God's way than about what people think of us, our actions will begin to change the world, and persecution will follow. But persecution is not the end of the story. The end of the story is the reality of God's kingdom coming upon the earth, God's will being done in us as it is in heaven.

When we recognize how much we need God, when we enter into life fully, when we use our powers under God's direction, when we hunger for God's way, when we love mercy, when we focus our heart on God, when we work for peace and give ourselves fully to what we believe in—every moment we are able to do these things, we walk the way of blessedness.

Daily Reflections for Week 8

Day 1—Read Jeremiah 28:1-4 and 29:1, 4-9.

The false prophet Hananiah said that the exile would be short and God's people would be home soon. Who in our time preaches an "easy" message, undemanding of listeners? Why would anyone do this?

Jeremiah tells the exiles to build houses, marry and have children, and pray for the city. What do you think Jeremiah's message means for you today?

In what sense are followers of Christ exiles, regardless of where they live?

What helps you live as one of God's people when those around you live by different values?

Day 2—Read John 15:18-21.

What kinds of people does the world "love"? Do you think the world loves some Christians? If so, what kind? How does this square with what Jesus says in this passage?

Jesus said that we do not belong to the world. Given the universal human yearning to feel that we belong, how do we build a sense of citizenship in the new world that God wants to establish?

Jesus said that persecution is inevitable. Have you experienced persecution because of your Christianity? How can people in the U.S. understand the emotions described here, since we live in a "Christian" nation?

In what areas do your Christian values differ from the values of our culture? How do your actions differ from the actions of non-Christians? In what ways do your values differ from the values of other Christians?

Day 3—Read 1 Peter 4:12-19.

How and where are Christians persecuted for their faith today? Have you known anyone from one of these places, and if so, what picture did they paint of the situation Christians face?

This passage says that when we suffer for Christ, the Spirit of God rests on us. Have you ever known someone on whom the Spirit of God rested? What evidence tells us that the Spirit of God rests on someone?

We are told here to entrust ourselves to "a faithful Creator, while continuing to do good." What helps you to continue doing what God asks when the going gets tough? What do you say to yourself in such times?

Day 4—Read Hebrews 11:1-8, 32-38.

What stories or character(s) from the Bible serve as a guide for your faith? What do you identify with that makes these important to you?

List three or four heroes and note an inspiring quality or action for each one. Are these heroes people of faith? What contemporary believers inspire you to want to follow Christ more faithfully?

Imagine yourself in a Roman arena facing lions, with other believers alongside you. What would you say and do to help one another? What does this suggest to you about how we can face suffering in our time?

Day 5—Read Colossians 1:24 and Philippians 1:27-29.

The verse from Colossians refers to "completing . . . Christ's afflictions." In what sense does Christ's suffering continue in our world? How do we become part of this suffering?

Wanting to avoid pain is natural. So what might help us see suffering for Christ as a privilege?

What can believers do to avoid being "intimidated by [our] opponents" (Phil. 1:28)? What specific things can we do to prepare ourselves to face times of suffering with faith?

Rewriting the Beatitude

Write here your restatement of this week's beatitude and an opposite "Cursed are . . ." or "Woe to . . ." statement:

Positive: _____ are those who

_____

_____.

Negative:

_____

_____.

Notes for Group Session

My response to this week's beatitude will be

_____

_____.

Leader's Guide for Group Sessions

INTRODUCTORY SESSION

Consider holding a short introductory meeting one week before the study begins to distribute books, talk about the format of the study, and establish a group covenant.

If your group does not have a preliminary meeting, allow time in the first session to discuss the format of the study and to agree on ground rules for the group. Thirty minutes should be adequate, but let participants know ahead of time that this meeting will last longer than an hour.

Points to Cover in Preliminary Meeting

1. Study format

Group members will read a short chapter before each session, so distribute books at least a week before the first session. Chapters can be read in about ten or fifteen minutes. Daily scripture reflection questions are provided for five days (not six or seven) each week; the time needed to complete these will vary by individual. Participants may write in their books or in a separate journal. What participants write in response to the scripture reflection will remain private; no one will see the books, and though they will be invited to talk about their responses at times, anyone may choose to pass (not speak) at any time.

2. Ground rules

Invite group members to agree on how they want the group to function. Many groups operate with agreements such as these:

*   Group members will attend unless pressing circumstances prevent.
*   Members will prepare for each week's session by reading/reflecting.

- Members will pray for one another between sessions.
- Members will speak from their own experience and refrain from giving advice.
- No one is ever forced to speak; anyone may say "pass" at any time in any activity or discussion. What is said in the group sessions is considered confidential; it stays there. Persons may talk about their experience in the group in other settings but not about others' comments.
- Meetings will begin and end on time.
- Members will show respect for differences by listening to one another without interrupting or arguing, even when opinions differ.

You may want to post your group covenant in the meeting room each week.

ABOUT THE SESSIONS

Each weekly session is designed to last about an hour. Each session includes:
- Lighting the Christ candle and Opening Prayer *(3 minutes)*
- Music/Singing *(5 minutes)*
- Reflection on Reading/Journaling/Personal Response *(10 minutes)*
- Discussion of Blessed/Cursed Paraphrases *(10–15 minutes)*
- "Moving Deeper" Activity *(15–20 minutes)*
- Commitment to Personal Response *(5 minutes)*
- Giving of Gifts *(2 minutes)*
- Closing Prayer *(5 minutes)*

Sessions do not require extensive leader preparation beyond reading each week's chapter and the daily scripture readings, responding to the daily reflection questions, and bringing/preparing reminder objects. *(See "Looking Ahead" for preparation needed for certain weeks.)* Each session recommends music that may be sung. If you do not have the gift of leading singing, recruit someone to do this for the group.

The Christ candle. A white pillar candle is often used as a Christ candle. You may want to create a worship center by placing the candle on a white cloth on a small table or somewhere that allows everyone to see it. If you like, add a cross or other symbolic or seasonal objects to the setting. As you light the candle, say, "We light this candle as a reminder that Christ is here with us and is a part of our conversations."

Opening Prayer. The opening prayer may be a standard prayer that the group prays together (see Session 1 for options) or a spontaneous prayer offered by the leader or a volunteer. Praying aloud a standard prayer to open each session helps build group identity. As the prayer becomes familiar, praying it together can help people settle into the session. If you plan to have a group member pray, ask someone you know feels comfortable praying in a group, or contact the person ahead of time. Many people find it difficult to pray aloud impromptu in a group but are happy to do so if given time beforehand to prepare.

Music/Singing. Each session plan suggests songs that the group may sing or listen to during the group meeting. Live music is best, if you have a pianist or guitarist available, but even singing along with a CD or DVD player adds to the group session. In addition to the vocal music, provide some soft, meditative instrumental music at the point in each session when participants consider their personal responses for the coming week. Recorded music is fine for this, and you may want to use the same music for all eight weeks.

Hymnal Abbreviations

United Methodist Hymnal—UMH

New Century Hymnal (United Church of Christ)—NCH

The Hymnal 1982 (Episcopal Church)—EH

The Presbyterian Hymnal—PH

Lutheran Book of Worship—LBW

The Faith We Sing—TFWS

Reflection on Reading/Journaling/Personal Response. After the opening prayer, each week's session begins with participants talking in groups of three about the week's reading and their journaling in response to the daily questions. Explain that no one will be forced to talk about the content of what he or she wrote in response to the journal questions. Group members may comment in general about the experience or choose to say nothing at all, but their journal remains completely private. No one else will see it or read it. Anyone may say "pass" in response to any question. At the end of each session, participants will be invited to consider committing to a personal response to the session. The next week, they will be invited to discuss their commitments with their group, again with the understanding that they may choose not to say anything.

Discussion of Blessed/Cursed Paraphrases. Each week the journaling exercises end with participants writing in their own words the week's beatitude and an opposite "curse" or "woe" as the form appears in Jeremiah 17:5-8 and Luke 6:20-26 (and other places in the Bible). Hearing these rewordings will inform the whole group of the varied meanings that can be derived from the Beatitudes; it will also help group members reflect on how Jesus' original hearers might have completed these sayings in their own thoughts. Some people may find the curses/woes part of the exercise difficult (not just because of the writing, though some will dislike that) because we are taught to be "nice." This process of looking at possible bad results is meant to make people think. If some have difficulty with the concept of writing and talking about these negatives, direct them to the book of Proverbs, especially chapter 10 with its many positive/negative pairings. The wisdom sayings in Proverbs are the most familiar makarisms and may help people to understand the form and to feel more comfortable with it.

Moving Deeper. Each session includes an exploration activity to allow participants to apply the content of the week's reading to their lives and to contemporary events and situations. The form of these activities varies from week to week. Some are quiet and meditative, while others are more interactive. Each session's plan includes detailed instructions. See "Preparing for This Session" for supplies needed.

Commitment to Personal Response. In each session, the leader asks group members to respond to a question or challenge. As quiet music plays, the leader invites each person to consider prayerfully and privately some action she or he will take in the coming week and to write it in the book at the place provided.

Giving of Gifts. Each week, the leader gives participants a small gift to carry with them during the week as a reminder of the beatitude just studied. For example, the first week ("Blessed are the poor in spirit"), the leader gives each person a penny taped to a three-by-five card on which a short message has been written or printed. See "Preparing for This Session" for information about each week's gift.

Closing Prayer. Closing prayer follows the same format each week. The leader invites group members first to voice prayer concerns growing out of the discussion of the week's material. Then the leader asks for intercessory concerns of the congregation or community. Closing prayer should be informal and personal, led by the session leader or a volunteer.

LOOKING AHEAD

Session 2: You will need several copies of the local and national/international sections of your newspaper(s) (not necessarily the same day) and copies of your church's weekly intercessory prayer list, if your church prepares such a list, for each group member.

Sessions 5 and 6: You will need copies of the spiritual gifts inventory and description/explanation of each gift from www.equippedforeverygoodwork.org. You can download these forms and print and photocopy them. **Hand out the inventories at the end of Session 5 so participants can complete them at home and bring them back in Session 6.** This is a self-scoring inventory. If you are unfamiliar with spiritual gifts terminology, consult some of the books listed in "For Further Reading" to prepare for the discussion in Session 6. For more information about personal mission statements, consult Stephen Covey's books listed in the same appendix, or go to the Franklin-Covey Web site, www.franklincovey.com, to the "Mission Statement Builder," an online guide to creating a personal mission statement.

Session 8: Invite a person of another faith who lives in this country or a Christian who has lived in a culture where Christians are a small minority (a country such as Saudi Arabia, Egypt, Indonesia, or India) to speak to the group about persecution because of personal faith or about limits on expression of faith. If you don't know anyone like this, ask church staff members or the group for suggestions of someone you might invite.

Extend the invitation as soon as possible to give the speaker time to prepare. Ask the person to speak for whatever length of time you feel is appropriate, allowing time for questions from the group. Be sure to tell the speaker there will be a question-and-answer opportunity. You may want to extend the meeting time for this session. Allow the group to discuss this possibility and to decide if you will meet for a longer time.

You will need small crosses (available at Christian bookstores) to give as the week's gift, one per participant.

SESSION 1: BLESSED ARE THE POOR IN SPIRIT

Supplies for This Session
- ☐ Christ candle/worship center materials
- ☐ Matches or candlelighter
- ☐ Chart-sized paper and markers or whiteboard and markers
- ☐ Hymnals and music leader (or recorded music and means to play it)
- ☐ Index cards on which you have printed one of the following prayers or a prayer you have written (if the group will use a standard opening).

Option 1: Blessed are we, O God, to know you and to be called your children. Open our ears to hear, our minds to understand, and our hearts to respond to what you will say to us in this time together. Amen.

Option 2: O God, to know you and to follow you is to be deeply blessed. Write your message to us ever more deeply on our hearts, that we may live as your transformed people and see the kingdoms of this world become the kingdom of our God. Amen.

Option 3: Dear God, all that we are, all that we have, we owe to your grace at work in us. Help us to live as your children, your heirs, that all the world may come to see the family likeness in us—in our words, our attitudes, and our actions. Amen.

☐ Bible

☐ For each participant, a three-by-five card with a penny glued below this message: All that I am and all that I have are an expression of God's grace working in my life.

Preparing for This Session

Read through the guided meditation on Luke 18:18-25 (in the section "Moving Deeper") to become familiar with it and to get a feel for how long the pauses for reflection need to be. When you read the meditation in the group session, read slowly. You may want to do the meditation yourself as you lead the group, using your experience as a guide to the timing of pauses. Allow pauses long enough for group members to develop images fully before moving to a new image. Otherwise, they may feel rushed or frustrated.

Lighting the Christ Candle

Distribute the cards printed with the opening prayer if the group will pray in unison. Invite the group members to quiet themselves. Then light the Christ candle, saying, "We light this candle as a reminder that Christ is here with us and is a part of our conversations."

Opening Prayer

If you are using the same prayer for each session, say, "Join me in the opening prayer printed on the card" and begin praying. Or have a volunteer pray, or pray a prayer of your own. (Collect the cards at the end of the session.)

Music/Singing

Play or sing "Seek Ye First" (#405, *UMH*; #333, *PH*).

Reflection on Reading/Journaling

Step 1. If this session is your group's first meeting, take time to review the format of the book and to remind group members that part of each week's session will include discussing responses to the journaling questions. If your group had an introductory session, remind them about this discussion step. Emphasize that no one will be required to reveal anything personal in these responses unless they choose to do so.

Step 2. If this session is your group's first meeting, review ground rules for discussion, emphasizing everyone's right to privacy and freedom to speak or refrain from speaking. If your group established ground rules in an earlier meeting, ask group members if they want to add other agreements about discussions.

Step 3. Ask if anyone in the group has experience with keeping a spiritual journal or writing personal responses to scripture, as this book directs. Invite those who have done so to say how they felt/feel about this process and what, if anything, they got out of it. Ask those who have not written in this way before or who have not found keeping a journal worthwhile to commit to trying the process for at least the next three weeks as an experiment of solidarity with the group.

Step 4. Ask participants to group themselves in threes. Remind them to allow each person an opportunity to respond to the questions before beginning any further discussion. Ask (or write on chart/board) these questions: "Did you highlight or underline passages in this week's reading? What caught your attention? How does this relate to your life?" Allow each person two minutes to respond.

Step 5. Ask (or write on chart/board): "Which daily scripture reflection did you find most challenging or most interesting? Why?" Allow each person two minutes to respond.

Discussion of Blessed/Cursed Paraphrases

Step 1. Direct participants to page 16, to the discussion of the "Blessed are/Cursed are" double statements in scripture. Ask if anyone has noticed this form or read about it before. If so, invite them to expand on this idea for the group. Ask if everyone understands the material about the opposite statements from Proverbs. If not, ask what their questions are, and invite group members to comment/answer/help them understand. Ask, "Can anyone help us with this?" Allow time for comments. If the questions are not resolved, encourage participants to listen to the next part of the activity to see if it answers the questions.

Step 2. Ask group members: "Did you find it difficult to rewrite this first beatitude? If so, what made the process tough for you? Or did you find it easy?" Allow time for responses.

Step 3. Ask: "Did you use 'Cursed are . . .' or 'Woe to . . .' to write your negative, and why did you choose the form that you did? How did you feel about writing a negative or opposite statement?" Allow time for responses.

Step 4. Ask: "Was writing a negative opposite more difficult than restating the beatitude, or was it easier? Why?" Allow time for responses.

Step 5. Ask, "Did writing an opposite to the beatitude lead you to any insights about it or about yourself?" Allow time for responses.

Step 6. Invite all who wrote negative restatements of the beatitude to read them, each person in turn. After all have read, ask for general comments about the ideas.

Step 7. Invite group members to read in turn their positive restatements.

Step 8. Tell participants that they will write these positive and negative restatements each week for that week's beatitude.

Moving Deeper: Guided Meditation on Luke 18:18-25

Step 1. Explain that you will lead the group in a meditation on the scripture story about the man whom Jesus told to sell all his possessions and give the money to the poor. Say: "Some of you may not have experienced guided meditation before. If not, try to relax and be open to this way of experiencing scripture. I will read the story from scripture one time to orient you to the story and then a second time more slowly. After that the guided meditation will begin. I will ask you to imagine yourself in the story, guiding you with suggestions and questions, pausing to allow you time to experience the story. There is no right or wrong outcome of a meditation like this. Just listen to the words as I read them and use your imagination to enter into the scene. This practice is called Ignatian meditation, after Saint Ignatius, who taught this way of listening to and interacting with scripture."

Step 2. Invite participants to make themselves comfortable. Ask them to sit with feet flat on the floor and backs well supported. Allow them to move to a more comfortable place in the room if they wish. Some people may want to sit or lie on the floor. Invite participants to take several deep breaths to quiet themselves. Suggest that they may find it easier to follow their imagination if they close their eyes while you read—and yes, it's okay if they fall asleep.

Step 3. Read aloud Luke 18:18-25. Then read it again, slowly, pausing where it seems natural.

Step 4. Read the guided meditation below, pausing at the ellipses (. . .) to allow time for participants to experience what you direct them to imagine.

Imagine that you are this man. You are successful—perhaps a city official or a professional person. You study the scripture and go to synagogue every Sabbath; you pray every day, as your father did before you. . . . You are serious about your faith, and you want to talk to Jesus. You need reassurance. . . . Imagine that you see him as you are walking through your village. How do you know that it is Jesus? What about him catches your attention? . . . You watch as he blesses some children . . . As they leave with their parents, Jesus is left alone. You begin to walk toward him. What do you feel? . . . What is the expression on Jesus' face? . . . Imagine the moment when he sees you approaching. His face lights up in welcome. . . .

You approach him, and Jesus smiles. . . . You tell him who you are and what you do to earn your living. . . . He listens, encouraging you to say more about yourself. . . .

As you talk with him, you sense within your heart a yearning, a desire to be sure. . . . You ask him the question that has been turning in your mind: "Good Teacher, what must I do to inherit eternal life?" Jesus looks at you. Allow yourself to see his face as he considers your question. . . .

Then he says, "You know the commandments: 'You shall not commit adultery; You shall not murder; You shall not steal; You shall not bear false witness; Honor your father and mother.'" You think about yourself, and you feel relieved. You are a good person. You want to obey God. You have tried to be honorable in your relationships. You haven't always been perfect, of course . . . . But you have worked at being a good person.

And so you say to him, "You know that I have kept all these commandments." Jesus looks at you with gentleness and kindness in his face. . . . He sighs, and after a few moments, he says to you, "One more thing: Give up all your possessions. Sell everything you have and give the money to the poor." . . . What do you feel? . . . What possessions do you think about first? . . . Which things do you feel willing to give up? . . . Are there some possessions that you want to hold back, maybe things you want to pass on to your children or grandchildren? . . . Are there some possessions—like your investments or retirement savings or a college fund—that you think Jesus might exempt from this request? . . . But he said, "Give up all your possessions." Does he really mean that you should let go of everything? Could he really mean every possession you own? . . .

As you think about Jesus' words, you begin to tally in your mind the value of your possessions: your home . . . your car or cars . . . all the electronic gadgets . . . the art and decorative things . . . jewelry . . . books and music . . . your clothing. . . . As you begin to consider doing what Jesus says, what feelings are you aware of ? . . .

What will you have left if you let go of all your possessions? Are you rich in other ways—in education or training? . . . in respect from others? . . . in relationships? . . . in talents or skills? . . . Which of *these* riches would you have a hard time letting go of? . . .

If all of your riches—possessions and other treasures—were gone tomorrow, who would you be? . . . What possibilities does that bring to mind? . . .

Finally, you must decide if you will do what Jesus asks. You make your decision . . . and you turn to walk away, your head bowed with sadness. . . . Why are you sad? Is it because you are going to do what Jesus asks? Or are you sad because you know you cannot do it? . . .

As you walk, let your thoughts come back to this place and this time. . . . What feelings and thoughts linger in you? . . . When you are ready, open your eyes.

Step 5. Direct participants to sit in silence for a minute after the meditation ends. Then invite them to write in their books/journals a short response to the meditation—anything they want to remember, any feelings or insights that came to them.

Commitment to Personal Response

Step 1. Start the meditative music. Tell participants that you will give them some time to consider what they experienced in this meditation about becoming poor. Allow one to two minutes for reflection.

Step 2. Invite the group to think about the contrast between being like the rich young ruler and being poor in spirit—absolutely dependent on God. Ask: "If being like the rich man were on one end of a continuum and being poor in spirit were on the other, where would you be—somewhere in the middle? closer to one end or the other?"

Step 3. Ask, "What is one small action you can take in the coming week to remind yourself to turn to God for everything?" Give participants time to think. Ask them to note that one small act in their journal or book.

Giving of Gifts

Distribute the cards with pennies and reminder sentence on them, one to each person. Ask group members to place the cards where they will see them daily this coming week—on their bathroom mirror, beside the telephone, on the computer monitor, on the refrigerator, or somewhere else they choose. Say, "This penny is a reminder that our own resources will never be enough to help us face life—but God's grace working in and through us is enough."

Closing Prayer

List prayer concerns on a board or chart. Ask first for concerns that arise from the discussion. You may want to begin with "For help from and reliance on God to keep the commitments we make." Then ask for community concerns. Ask for a volunteer to pray, or you may pray.

Sending Forth

Say, "Go in peace, knowing that God's grace working in you is enough."

SESSION 2: BLESSED ARE THOSE WHO MOURN

Supplies for This Session
- ☐ Christ candle/worship center materials
- ☐ Matches or candlelighter
- ☐ Chart-sized paper and markers or whiteboard and markers
- ☐ Hymnals and music leader (or recorded music and means to play it)
- ☐ Local sections of newspaper(s), enough for each person to have a section or several pages
- ☐ Prayer concerns list from your congregation for each group member

Preparing for This Session

If your church keeps a list of prayer concerns, get a copy for each group member. If there is no printed list of concerns, make notes during the Sunday service or call the church/pastor to find out special needs in your congregation. From this, create a list of concerns to hand out at the end of the session.

Lighting the Christ Candle

Distribute the cards printed with the opening prayer if it is to be prayed in unison. Invite the group members to quiet themselves. Then light the Christ candle, saying, "We light this candle as a reminder that Christ is here with us and is a part of our conversations."

Opening Prayer

Say, "Join me in the opening prayer printed on the card" and begin praying. Or ask the person you invited ahead of time to pray, or pray your own prayer. (Collect the cards at the end of the session for use in future weeks.)

Music/Singing

Sing "Spirit Song" (#347, *UMH*) or "Here I Am, Lord" (#593, *UMH*; #525, *PH*).

Reflection on Reading/Journaling/Personal Response Commitments

Step 1. Ask participants to form groups of three. Invite individuals to comment within their groups on how they did with their personal response, whatever they committed to do. Say: "You may say, 'I completely forgot about it once I left here,' or, 'I discovered that what I said I'd do was impossible.' No one will keep score. This is just a way of checking in. And you don't have to say much. You'll have only one minute each." Allow each person one minute to respond.

Step 2. Remain in groups of three. Remind participants to allow each person an opportunity to respond to the questions before beginning any further discussion. Ask (or write on chart/board) these questions: "Did you highlight or underline passages in this week's reading? What caught your attention? How does this relate to your life?" Allow each person two minutes to respond.

Step 3. Ask (or write on chart/board): "Which daily scripture reflection did you find most challenging or most interesting? Why?" Allow each person two minutes to respond.

Discussion of Blessed/Cursed Paraphrases

(If the group is large, you may subdivide to do steps 1–3 of this activity. If there are eight or fewer participants, the group as a whole can do the steps together.)

Step 1. Invite group members to find their rewritten beatitude in their journals or books. Ask: "Did you find it difficult to rewrite this week's beatitude?

Was it easier or harder this week than last?" Allow time for responses.

Step 2. Ask, "Did writing an opposite to this beatitude lead you to any insights about it or about yourself?" Allow time for responses.

Step 3. Invite all who wrote negative restatements of the beatitude to read them, each person in turn. After all have read, ask for general comments about the ideas.

Step 4. Invite group members to read in turn their positive restatements of the beatitude. After all have read, ask what ideas in the restatements members found helpful.

Step 5. Ask the group to point out places where they hear consensus or similar ideas in the restatements of the beatitude. If time permits, construct a group restatement of "Blessed are those who mourn, for . . ." from all the individual statements.

Moving Deeper

Step 1. Distribute the newspaper sections so each person has one.

Step 2. Write on the board/chart: "Where in these news accounts do you see situations over which you think people mourn? Where do you see situations over which God must mourn?" Allow five minutes for group members to scan the newspapers.

Step 3. Divide a piece of chart paper/board into two columns. Invite group members to mention the situations they find over which people mourn. As group members speak, have someone list in the left column on the chart/board the individual items.

Step 4. Ask, "How does or might God's comfort come to these people?" As group members respond, have someone record the responses in the right column of the chart/board.

Step 5. On another piece of chart/board divided into two columns, list in the left column situations over which God mourns. In the right column, list ways that individuals and the congregation as a whole might respond or already respond to these situations that grieve God.

Commitment to Personal Response

Step 1. Start the meditative music. Direct participants to be silent and wait to see if one of the situations mentioned in the preceding activity calls forth some response from them.

Step 2. After two or three minutes, direct group members to write in their journals/books about one of these situations (or another not listed) that tugs at their heart, about which they might say, "Someone should do something about that!"

Step 3. Ask them to answer these questions: "What could I do to be an instrument of God's comfort in this situation in the coming week? What keeps me from responding? How can I free myself to respond?"

Step 4. Ask participants to write in their journal/book how they will respond to one of these situations between now and the next meeting.

Giving of Gifts

Give each participant a copy of your church's intercessory prayer list or a list of concerns mentioned in the previous Sunday's service. Ask them to place this where it will remind them to be open during this week to receive and to give God's comfort.

Closing Prayer

After asking for mention of concerns arising from the discussion and for personal requests for prayer, ask for a volunteer to pray spontaneously. Or you may pray this prayer or another:

> O God, we are grateful that you weep with each one of us when we weep. Help us to open ourselves to receive your comfort for ourselves. And give us love and strength to be instruments of your comfort by caring tenderly for those who are in need right now. We pray especially for _____ *(name specific persons and needs mentioned by group members)*. By your grace, fill us with joy even in times of struggle and sorrow. We pray in Christ's name. Amen.

Sending Forth

Say, "Go in peace, in the company of our God, who invites us to live all of life fully."

SESSION 3: BLESSED ARE THE MEEK

Supplies for This Session

☐ Christ candle/worship center materials
☐ Matches or candlelighter
☐ Chart-sized paper and markers or whiteboard and markers
☐ Hymnals and music leader (or recorded music and means to play it)
☐ Sticky notes or three-by-five cards to create a mock to-do list for each person (gift for this session)

Preparing for This Session

1. Read through the directions for the "Moving Deeper" activity until you feel comfortable leading it.
2. Create mock daily to-do lists, one per person. List the numbers 1–5 vertically on a sticky note or a three-by-five card. Beside #1, write, "Spend two minutes listening for God's voice."

Lighting the Christ Candle

Distribute the cards printed with the opening prayer if it will be prayed in unison. Invite the group members to quiet themselves. Then light the Christ candle, saying, "We light this candle as a reminder that Christ is here with us and is a part of our conversations."

Opening Prayer

If you are using the same prayer for each session, say, "Join me in the opening prayer printed on the card," and begin praying. (Collect the cards at the end of the session for use in future weeks.) Or ask the person you invited ahead of time to pray, or pray a prayer of your own.

Music/Singing

Sing "Take My Life and Let It Be" (No. 399, *UMH*; No. 391, *PH*; No. 406, *LBW*; No. 707, *EH*; No. 448, *NCH*).

Reflection on Reading/Journaling/Personal Response Commitments

Step 1. Ask participants to group themselves in threes. Remind the groups to give each person opportunity to respond to the questions before beginning any further discussion. Invite persons to comment within their groups on how they did with their personal response, whatever they committed to do. Remind them that no one will keep score; this is just a way of checking in. Allow each person one minute to respond.

Step 2. Ask (or write on chart/board) these questions: "Did you highlight or underline passages in this week's reading? What caught your attention? How does this relate to your life?" Allow each person two minutes to respond.

Step 3. Ask (or write on chart/board): "Which daily scripture reflection did you find most challenging or most interesting? Why?" In the groups, allow each person two minutes to respond.

Discussion of Blessed/Cursed Paraphrases

(If the group is large, you may subdivide to do steps 1–3 of this activity. If there are eight or fewer participants, the entire group can do the steps together.)

Step 1. Invite group members to get out their journals/books and find their rewritten beatitude. Ask: "Did you find it difficult to rewrite this week's beatitude? Was it easier or harder this week than last?" Allow time for responses.

Step 2. Ask, "Did writing an opposite to this beatitude lead you to any insights about it or about yourself?" Allow time for responses.

Step 3. Invite all who wrote negative restatements of the beatitude to take turns reading them. After all have read, ask for general comments about the ideas.

Step 4. Invite group members to read in turn their positive restatements of the beatitude. After all have read, ask what ideas in the restatements members found helpful.

Step 5. Ask the group to point out places where they hear consensus or similar ideas in the restatements of the beatitude. If time permits, consider constructing a group restatement of "Blessed are the meek, for . . . " from all the individual statements.

Moving Deeper

Leader: This week's activity is about doing nothing (to state a paradox). It will allow participants to respond to a fairly familiar scripture passage on different levels. Then you will guide a discussion (questions provided here) about the feelings this exercise elicits and why many of us have difficulty "doing nothing."

The experience centers on responding to Psalm 46:10, "Be still, and know that I am God." This will be a time of silent reflection. Invite group members to think during the silence about the phrases from the psalm. Reassure them that no response is right or wrong; they are simply to allow themselves to consider the words of the psalm and the feelings that arise as they do so.

Step 1. Ask group members to get comfortable, with feet flat on the floor and backs supported.

Step 2. Ask them to take several deep breaths to quiet themselves. Invite them to close their eyes as an aid to concentration.

Step 3. Say each of these phrases, pausing for ninety seconds to two minutes of silence after each one:

"Be still, and know that I am God!"

"Be still, and know that I am . . ."

"Be still, and know . . ."

"Be still . . ."

"Be . . ."

Step 4. Invite group members to take a few moments to write in their books/journals their thoughts and feelings about this process.

Step 5. Ask:"Does anyone want to comment on the exercise? How did you feel about sitting in silence for so long?" Allow time for responses.

Step 6. Ask, "Was it easier for you to think about 'Be still, and know that I am God!' than to think about just 'Be'?" Allow time for responses.

Step 7. Ask: "In what ways does our culture pressure people more toward doing and accomplishing than toward taking time simply to 'be'? Do you agree that we value doing more than being?" Allow time for responses.

Step 8. Ask: "What about the church—does it teach more about doing or about being? Is there pressure toward one more than the other?" Allow time for responses.

Commitment to Personal Response

Step 1. Start the meditative music. Tell participants that you are going to give them some time to consider their response to this week's session.

Step 2. Say: "After the readings, daily reflections, and discussion, where do you see yourself in relation to how you use your powers and how you refrain from using them? Are there situations and relationships where you need to assert yourself more? Are there situations and relationships where you need to refrain from using your powers?" Allow a minute or two of silence for reflection.

Step 3. Say, "In the coming week, where do you want to become more aware of how you are responding?" Allow a minute or two of silence for reflection.

Step 4. Ask, "What can you do to remind yourself in these situations and relationships to pause before responding so that you can listen for direction from God about how to use your powers?" Allow a minute for reflection.

Step 5. Invite participants to note in their books/journals what they will do in the coming week to give attention to how they use their powers.

Giving of Gifts

Give each participant a copy of the "Daily To-Do List" and encourage group members to place it where they will see it each day of the coming week. Explain that the to-do list reminds us that sometimes not acting is what God wills and that each of us must listen for God's direction to know when we need to act and when we need to refrain from acting.

Closing Prayer

Invite group members to voice concerns that come from this session's content and to mention personal concerns. Ask for a volunteer to pray, lead a closing prayer of your own creation, or pray this prayer:

> God of all power, during this week, nudge us when you want us to use our powers, and help us to know when you want us to refrain from acting or speaking. Help us to be faithful and to place our powers under your control. We entrust to your love and power the concerns we have named here. We bring to you _____ *(name specific persons and needs mentioned by group members)*. Amen.

Sending Forth

Say, "Go in the knowledge that God has given you your powers and will help you to use them wisely."

SESSION 4: BLESSED ARE THOSE WHO HUNGER AND THIRST FOR RIGHTEOUSNESS

Supplies for This Session

☐ Christ candle/worship center materials
☐ Matches or candlelighter
☐ Chart-sized paper and markers or whiteboard and markers
☐ Hymnals and music leader (or recorded music and means to play it)
☐ Legal-size (8½ by 14) paper, a few sheets for each participant
☐ Pencils
☐ Individual salt packets (available from fast-food restaurants), one per participant
☐ Dried beans
☐ Plastic snack bags with seals

Preparing for This Session

Using plastic snack bags, create a reminder gift for each participant, putting a salt packet and a few beans in each bag. (Note: Please don't take these salt packets from a fast-food restaurant without asking; tell the manager how many you need and why. Managers are usually happy to help a church group.) Read through the "Moving Deeper" activity until you are familiar with the process it outlines and feel comfortable leading it.

Lighting the Christ Candle

Distribute the cards printed with the opening prayer if it is to be prayed in unison. Invite the group members to quiet themselves. Light the Christ candle, saying, "We light this candle as a reminder that Christ is here with us and is a part of our conversations."

Opening Prayer

Say, "Join me in the opening prayer printed on the card" and begin praying; or, if your group is not using the same prayer each week, ask the person you invited ahead of time to pray, or lead a prayer yourself. (Collect the cards at the end of the session for use in future weeks.)

Music/Singing

Sing "As the Deer"(No. 2025, *TFWS*) or the chorus "With All My Heart" if you know it.

Reflection on Reading/Journaling/Personal Response Commitments

Step 1. Ask participants to group themselves in threes. Remind the groups to allow each person an opportunity to respond to the questions before beginning any further discussion. Invite individuals to comment within their groups on how they did with their personal response, whatever they committed to do. Remind them that no one is keeping score and that this is just a way of checking in. Allow each person one minute to respond.

Step 2. Ask (or write on the chart/board) these questions: "What passages in this week's reading did you highlight or underline? What caught your attention? How does this relate to your life?" Allow each person two minutes to respond.

Step 3. Ask (or write on the chart/board): "Which daily scripture reflection did you find most challenging or most interesting? Why?" In the groups, allow each person two minutes to respond.

Discussion of Blessed/Cursed Paraphrases

(If the group is large, you may subdivide to do steps 1–3 of this activity. If there are eight or fewer participants, the entire group can do the steps together.)

Step 1. Invite group members to find their rewritten beatitude in their journals or books. Ask: "Did you find it difficult to rewrite this week's beatitude? Was it easier or harder this week than last?" Allow time for responses.

Step 2. Ask, "Did writing an opposite to this beatitude lead you to any insights about it or about yourself?" Allow time for responses.

Step 3. Invite all who wrote negative restatements of the beatitude to take turns reading them. After all have read, ask for general comments about the ideas.

Step 4. Invite group members to take turns reading their positive restatements of the beatitude. After all have read, ask what ideas in the restatements members found helpful.

Step 5. Ask the group to point out places where they hear consensus or similar ideas in the restatements of the beatitude. If time permits, construct a group restatement of "Blessed are those who hunger and thirst for righteousness . . ." from all the individual statements.

Moving Deeper

Step 1. On the board or on chart-sized paper, create two columns. Label one column "Personal Spiritual Practices" and the other "Ways of Serving."

Step 2. Invite group members to help you list various spiritual practices that help people be fed and grow spiritually—prayer (various kinds: intercessory, contemplative, breath prayers, etc.), Bible study, accountability/covenant groups, listening to music, listening to sermons/teaching, memorizing scripture, keeping a journal, going on retreats, having a spiritual director or spiritual friend/prayer partner, and so on. List as many as the group can come up with.

Step 3. Invite group members to do the same with ways of serving, defining service as anything done in God's name. Remind the group to consider invisible or private acts/ways of serving that may be overlooked, such as visiting persons who are confined at home, taking food to a sick neighbor, sending cards to those who are ill, giving money to community causes and the church, volunteering in the church thrift store or food pantry, and so. If they need help, refer them to Luke 4:18 and Matthew 25:31-46 for lists that Christ gave to outline areas of ministry.

Step 4. Explain that group members will create a time line of their life and spiritual growth. Hand out the 8½ by 14 paper and pencils. Ask them to draw a line across the 14-inch width of the paper, in the middle of the sheet. Then have them place tick marks along the line to indicate the decades of their life, with decade dates—1950, 1960, 1970, 1980, and so on. Above the line, ask them to record three or four events and activities of each decade.

Step 5. Invite group members to reflect. Say, "As you look at your time line, can you identify times of particular spiritual growth in your life?" After about two minutes of silence, ask them to draw stars or make some other special mark along their time lines to indicate these points.

Step 6. Ask the group members, "Which of the items on our lists—either personal practices or ways of serving—were a part of your life during these times of growth?" Ask them to list these below the line at the points where they placed the special mark.

Step 7. Ask group members to find a partner and exchange lists.

Step 8. Instruct group members to look at their partner's time line and see if they notice anything particular in the list about activities or involvements in the times of spiritual growth—a pattern, departures from a pattern, anything that they want to comment on to the person who created the time line. Allow five minutes for people to assess their partner's time line.

Step 9. Ask participants to take one minute each to comment to their partners about anything they see.

Step 10. Have everyone return the time lines to their creators. Then ask: "Did any of you realize anything or hear anything about yourself—not about your partner—regarding your spiritual growth that you'd like to comment on to the group? Were there any insights and surprises here for you?" Allow time for responses.

Commitment to Personal Response

Step 1. Start the meditative music. Tell participants that you are going to give them some time to consider their response to this week's session.

Step 2. Ask, "What can you do in the coming week to receive the spiritual food God offers you?"

Step 3. Ask: "Is there some new spiritual practice that you want to experience this week? What new way of listening to God do you want to try?" Allow a minute or so of silence.

Step 4. Invite participants to note in their journal/book what they intend to do in the coming week as a response to the session.

Giving of Gifts

Give each participant a gift bag. Say to them, "Carry this with you in the coming week to remind you to pay attention to your hunger and thirst for God and to remind you that God promises to feed us as we long for ourselves and the world to be put right."

Closing Prayer

Invite group members to mention prayer concerns arising from the session and other concerns. Ask for a volunteer to pray, lead a closing prayer of your own creation, or pray this prayer:

> O God, source of every good and perfect gift, thank you for placing our hungers and thirst within us to draw us to you. Just as you feed us in body and spirit day by day, hear our prayers for these concerns. We bring to you _____ (*name specific persons and needs mentioned by group members*). Provide what each person needs, what each situation requires. We ask you to feed and care for us and all those dear to us, and we give thanks that you promise to do so. Amen.

Sending Forth

Say, "Go in peace, knowing that God, who places our hungers within us, will feed us."

SESSION 5: BLESSED ARE THE MERCIFUL

Supplies for This Session

☐ Christ candle/worship center materials
☐ Matches or candlelighter
☐ Chart-sized paper and markers or whiteboard and markers
☐ Hymnals and music leader (or recorded music and means to play it)
☐ A small mirror or mirror tile (from home improvement store) for each participant (this week's gift)
☐ Copies of the spiritual gifts inventory and description of spiritual gifts (see second paragraph under "Looking Ahead," p. 115) for each participant.
☐ Prepare four slips of paper with the directions below. Fold each one and place the slips in an envelope or box.

Group 1: You are the woman taken "in the very act" and brought to Jesus. It is fifteen years later. How did you get involved with the man with whom you committed adultery? Talk about what happened when you were brought to Jesus. How were you different after that day? Did you ever see the man—the one who wasn't dragged before Jesus—again? What happened to your relationship with him? What about your marriage? How was it different after that day? How are you different today because of what Jesus said and did?

Group 2: You are the man who also committed adultery, the one whom the crowd didn't bring to Jesus. But somehow Jesus found out who you were and sought you out later that day. What did he say to you? What did you say to him? Did you try to continue your relationship with the woman? If so, what happened? If not, why not? Did this episode change anything about your behavior toward your wife? Looking back on that day fifteen years ago, what would you say to other men?

Group 3: You represent someone in the crowd who was eager to bring the woman before Jesus and who was the last one to drift away after Jesus wrote in the sand. Why did you bring the woman but not the adulterous man to Jesus? Why did you want her to be dealt with publicly? How did you feel when Jesus let her off so easily? Looking back, do you understand why he did what he did? In the fifteen years since this happened, have you ever participated in any other public censure or punishment again? Why or why not? What did Jesus write in the sand that made you finally leave? How are you different because of what happened that day?

Group 4: You represent someone who was reluctant to be part of bringing the woman without also bringing the man, but you went along with the crowd. You were also one of the first to leave after Jesus said, "Let the one who is without sin among you throw the first stone at her." Why did you go along with the crowd in spite of your reluctance? What did you feel when you saw what Jesus was writing in the sand? What did he write, anyway? Did you ever take part in a public censure like this again? How are you different because of what happened that day?

Preparing for This Session

Familiarize yourself with the spiritual gifts inventory in case anyone has questions. Look at the descriptions of gifts (www.equippedforeverygoodwork.org) and the list of service opportunities on pages 154–59 to see how different ways of serving fit with the descriptions of the gifts.

Lighting the Christ Candle

Distribute the cards printed with the opening prayer. Invite the group members to quiet themselves. Then light the Christ candle, saying, "We light this candle as a reminder that Christ is here with us and is a part of our conversations."

Opening Prayer

Say, "Join me in the opening prayer printed on the card" and begin praying; or, if your group is not using the same prayer each week, ask the person you invited ahead of time to pray, or lead a prayer yourself. (Collect the cards at the end of the session for use in future weeks.)

Music/Singing

Sing "Help Us Accept Each Other" (#560, *UMH*; #358, *PH*, #388, *NCH*) or "They'll Know We Are Christians by Our Love" (No. 2223, *TFWS*).

Reflection on Reading/Journaling/Personal Response Commitments

Step 1. Invite persons to comment within their groups on how it went with their personal response, whatever they committed to do. Remind them that no one is keeping score and that this is just a way of checking in. Allow each person one minute to respond.

Step 2. Ask participants to group themselves in threes. Remind them to allow each person an opportunity to respond to the questions before beginning any further discussion. Ask (or write on the chart/board) these questions: "Did you highlight or underline passages in this week's reading? What caught your attention? How does this relate to your life?" Allow each person two minutes to respond.

Step 3. Ask (or write on the chart/board): "Which daily reflection did you find most challenging or most interesting? Why?" In the groups, allow each person two minutes to respond.

Discussion of Blessed/Cursed Paraphrases

(If the group is large, you may subdivide to do steps 1–3 of this activity. If there are eight or fewer participants, the group as a whole can do the steps together.)

Step 1. Invite group members to get out their journals/books to find their rewritten beatitude. Ask: "Did you find it difficult to rewrite this week's beatitude? Was it easier or harder this week than last?" Allow time for responses.

Step 2. Ask, "Did writing an opposite to this beatitude lead you to any insights about it or about yourself?" Allow time for responses.

Step 3. Invite all who wrote negative restatements of the beatitude to read them, each person in turn. After all have read, ask for general comments about the ideas.

Step 4. Invite group members to read in turn their positive restatements of the beatitude. After all have read, ask what ideas in the restatements members found helpful.

Step 5. Ask the group to point out places where they hear consensus or similar ideas in the restatements of the beatitude. If time permits, construct a group restatement of "Blessed are the merciful . . ." from all the individual statements.

Moving Deeper

Step 1. Form four groups. Say: "We are going to revisit the story from John 8 of the woman taken in adultery. Each group will represent one character from the story. I will give each group a slip of paper with directions for what your small group will talk about. After the groups talk, we will reconvene; and I'll tell you what we're going to do next."

Step 2. Have a person in each group draw a slip from a box or envelope. Tell the groups they will have five minutes to talk. They are not to let the other groups know what they're talking about.

Step 3. After the groups have had time to talk, tell them that you are going to do a Jerry Springer/Ricki Lake-type interview panel with four people from the Bible story. Ask each group to choose someone to represent its character and its ideas/discussion, or you may choose someone. (The bigger the ham, the better.) Send the "adulterous man" off stage. Pull out three chairs and invite the woman and two people from the crowd to take a seat. You will be the host; the remaining group members will be the audience.

Step 4. Quietly tell the four people to interrupt and contradict one another as they wish, in the spirit of the free-for-all atmosphere of the show. Introduce the panel members one by one, using the content of the first sentence from each slip of paper: "Our guests today are Miriam Goldschmidt, the woman caught in the act of adultery and brought to Jesus fifteen years ago; Jeremiah Lieberman, someone in the crowd who was eager to bring the woman before Jesus and was one of the last to drift away after Jesus wrote in the sand; and David Smith, who felt reluctant about bringing the woman without also bringing the man— but went along with the crowd." Welcome them and thank them for agreeing to be here today.

Step 5. Begin with the woman. Ask her what she felt that day and how her marriage changed after that day. Ask if that was her last extramarital affair, and if so, why.

Step 6. Ask the reluctant crowd member one of the questions that group discussed. Then ask the eager crowd member one of that group's questions. (See step 7 for which questions not to ask yet.)

Step 7. Ask, "How are you different?/What has happened to you since that day?" and allow panel members to respond as they wish.

Step 8. Say, "We have a surprise guest, Eli Cohen, the man who also committed adultery but wasn't brought to Jesus." When he comes in, ask him about his meeting and conversation with Jesus.

Step 9. Thank the panel members for being with you and for helping the audience think about how the events of that day fifteen years earlier changed them. Invite the audience to thank them too, and end the "show."

Commitment to Personal Response

Step 1. Start the meditative music. Tell participants that you are going to give them some time to consider their response to this week's session.

Step 2. Invite group members to think of times they have received mercy and grace when they could have received punishment or censure. Allow two minutes of silence for reflection.

Step 3. Ask, "What do you want to say to God about this?" Allow a minute for prayer.

Step 4. Invite group members to think of situations or roles in which they could extend either mercy or judgment. Suggest a few: in traffic, in the grocery store, with coworkers, with their children. Allow a minute for reflection. Say, "How can you remember in those situations to show mercy while loving justice?" Allow a minute for reflection.

Step 5. Ask group members to note in their journal/book the commitment they want to make for the coming week.

Giving of Gifts

Give the mirrors to the participants and say: "These are to remind us of Jesus' words, 'Let anyone . . . who is without sin be the first to throw a stone.' We can look at ourselves in our mirror or think of this verse when we are tempted to deal harshly with anyone."

Note: Hand out the spiritual gifts inventory and ask group members to complete theirs and score it before the next session. Ask them to bring their inventory with them to Session 6.

Closing Prayer

Invite group members to mention prayer concerns arising from the session and other concerns. Ask for a volunteer to pray, lead a closing prayer of your own creation, or pray this prayer:

> O God, your mercy fills the earth. Make us like you, ready to pardon and be gentle with those who have stumbled, as you are gentle with us. Extend your grace and mercy to _____ *(name specific needs and situations)*. Help us in this week to show your mercy in all our dealings. Amen.

Sending Forth

Say, "Go in peace, offering mercy to all you meet in gratitude for all the mercy you have received."

SESSION 6: BLESSED ARE THE PURE IN HEART

Supplies for This Session

☐ Christ candle/worship center materials
☐ Matches or candlelighter
☐ Chart-sized paper and markers or whiteboard and markers
☐ Hymnals and music leader (or recorded music and means to play it)
☐ A small box, gift-wrapped, for each participant, with a To/From tag. Beside *To,* write the person's name. Beside *From,* write *God.* Because they symbolize individual constellations of spiritual gifts, the gift boxes should be various sizes and be wrapped in different designs of paper.
☐ Two copies of the list of "Service Opportunities" for each group member (Photocopy the list on pages 154–59, or go to www.upperroom.org/book-store/downloads/FocusedHeart.pdf for a printer-friendly PDF file.)

Preparing for This Session

To learn more about spiritual gifts, consult the books listed in "For Further Reading" (p. 151) or visit the Web site www.equippedforeverygoodwork.org to find out more about the inventory and the research behind it. However, you need not be an expert to lead the session.

Lighting the Christ Candle

Distribute the cards printed with the opening prayer. Invite the group members to quiet themselves. Then light the Christ candle, saying, "We light this candle as a reminder that Christ is here with us and is a part of our conversations."

Opening Prayer

Say, "Join me in the opening prayer printed on the card" and begin praying. If your group is not using the same prayer each week, ask the person you invited ahead of time to pray, or lead a prayer yourself. (Collect the cards at the end of the session for use in future sessions.)

Music/Singing

Sing "Change My Heart, O God" (#2152, *TFWS*) or "Be Thou My Vision" (#451, *UMH*; #339, *PH*; #451, *NCH*).

Reflection on Reading/Journaling/Personal Response Commitments

Step 1. Ask participants to group themselves in threes. Remind them to allow each person an opportunity to respond to the questions before beginning any further discussion. Invite individuals to comment within their groups on how it went with their personal response to last week's session, whatever they committed to do. Remind them that no one is keeping score and that this is just a way of checking in. Allow each person one minute to respond.

Step 2. Ask (or write on the chart/board) these questions: "Did you highlight or underline passages in this week's reading? What caught your attention? How does this relate to what's going on in your life right now?" Allow each person two minutes to respond.

Step 3. Ask (or write on the chart/board), "Which daily scripture reflection did you find most challenging or most interesting? Why?" In the groups, allow each person two minutes to respond.

Discussion of Blessed/Cursed Paraphrases

If the group is large, you may subdivide to do steps 1–3 of this activity. If you have eight or fewer participants, the entire group can do the steps together.

Step 1. Invite group members to get out their journals/books to find their rewritten beatitude. Ask: "Did you find it difficult to rewrite this week's beatitude? Was it easier or harder this week than last?"

Step 2. Ask, "Did writing an opposite to this beatitude lead you to any insights about it or about yourself?" Allow time for responses.

Step 3. Invite all who wrote negative restatements of the beatitude to read them, each person in turn. After all have read, ask for general comments about the ideas.

Step 4. Invite group members to read in turn their positive restatements of the beatitude. After all have read, ask what ideas in the restatements members found helpful.

Step 5. Ask the group to point out places where they hear consensus or similar ideas in the restatements of the beatitude. If time permits, construct a group restatement of "Blessed are the pure in heart . . . " from all the individual statements.

Moving Deeper

Step 1. Tell participants that we are going to look at spiritual gifts, individual purpose statements, and how these match up with ways of serving. Ask them to form groups of four.

Step 2. Ask group members to take the Service Opportunities list and place a check mark beside three or four tasks they have done and really enjoyed. Ask them to circle three or four tasks they have done but did not enjoy.

Step 3. Ask group members to open their books to Day 3's reflection (p. 86) where they wrote a purpose statement about themselves, "The Lord God has given me the _____ of a _____, that I might _____ the _____."

Step 4. Ask the groups to spend time responding to each group member in turn. Person #1 (the person closest to you in each group) will read the sentence about himself/herself. Someone in the group will then ask, "Would that have helped you say no to any of the invitations to do the things you have circled on your list?" If the person answers yes, ask, "How can you use your purpose statement to help you see where to use your gifts in the future?" If the person answers no, ask group members to suggest ways the statement might be more specific, following the guidelines on pages 82–83.

Step 5. Repeat step 4 for the other three persons in each group.

Step 6. If you have time, divide the Service Opportunities list among the groups and ask each group to match up the tasks on their portion of the list with the spiritual gifts that seem to fit with these tasks. If time permits, ask participants to comment on anything they noticed about the tasks and their own spiritual gifts.

Commitment to Personal Response

Step 1. Start the meditative music. Tell participants that you are going to give them some time to consider their personal response to this session.

Step 2. Invite group members to think of their individual purpose statement. Ask them to think about new possibilities they see for using their gifts.

Step 3. Invite group members to consider tasks they are involved in that don't fit with their purpose statement and their primary gifts. Allow a minute for reflection. Ask, "What tasks can you give up in order to free yourself for what God is calling you to do?" Allow a minute for reflection.

Step 4. Invite participants to note in their journal/book any insight or commitment they want to make.

Giving of Gifts

Give each person her/his small gift-wrapped box, saying, "This represents the gifts for ministry that God has given you. Place it on your dresser or in some other place where you will see it often. It serves as your reminder that God doesn't call anyone to do everything, but God does call each of us to do something. Identifying your spiritual gifts and refining your purpose statement will guide you to your personal 'something.'"

Closing Prayer

Invite group members to mention prayer concerns. Ask for a volunteer to pray, lead a closing prayer of your own creation, or pray this prayer:

> O God, thank you for making us all so different and so wonderful. Thank you for designing us so that using our spiritual gifts brings us deep joy. Show each of us where you want us to use our time and energy, that we may say yes when we need to say yes and no when we need to say no. Help us to serve you with a focused and pure heart. We ask your blessing on each member of this group and on those who need our prayers, especially _____ (name specific persons and needs mentioned by group members). Amen.

Sending Forth

Say, "Go in confidence, knowing that your gifts are exactly what you need to do what God calls you to do."

Session 7: Blessed Are the Peacemakers . . .

Supplies for This Session

☐ Christ candle/worship center materials
☐ Matches or candlelighter
☐ Chart-sized paper and markers or whiteboard and markers
☐ Hymnals and music leader (or recorded music and means to play it)
☐ Assorted adhesive bandages, one per participant (adhesive bandages printed with cartoon characters are memorable)
☐ A list of your congregation's outreach/service ministries for each participant (Be sure that it includes community outreaches such as daycare centers and service projects, as well as domestic and international missions activities.)
☐ A copy of your local newspaper, local and national/international sections

Preparing for This Session

Look through the newspaper and identify some places of brokenness in your community and in the world so you can be ready to point these out to the group.

Looking ahead: Confirm next week's special speaker. Ask if any special room arrangement is needed, and agree on where and when you (or some designee) will meet the speaker to escort him/her to the meeting place. Ask for a résumé or how the speaker prefers to be introduced to the group. If someone in the group knows the speaker personally, invite that person to greet the speaker and introduce him/her to the group. Let the speaker know the time limit and that the group will continue meeting after the speaker's time ends.

Lighting the Christ Candle

Distribute the cards printed with the opening prayer. Invite the group members to quiet themselves. Then light the Christ candle, saying, "We light this candle as a reminder that Christ is here with us and is a part of our conversations."

Opening Prayer

Say, "Join me in the opening prayer printed on the card" and begin praying. If the group does not use the same prayer each week, ask the person you invited ahead of time to pray, or lead a prayer yourself. (Collect the cards for use next week.)

Music/Singing

Sing "Let There Be Peace on Earth" (#431, *UMH*) or "Help Us Accept Each Other" (#560, *UMH*; #358, *PH*; #388, *NCH*).

Reflection on Reading/Journaling/Personal Response Commitments

Step 1.   Invite persons to comment within their groups on how it went with their personal response, whatever they committed to do. Remind them that no one is keeping score and that this is just a way of checking in. Allow each person one minute to respond.

Step 2.   Ask participants to group themselves in threes. Remind them to give each person opportunity to respond to the questions before beginning any further discussion. Ask (or write on chart/board) these questions: "Did you highlight or underline passages in this week's reading? What caught your attention? How does this relate to your life?" Allow each person two minutes to respond

Step 3.   Ask (or write on chart/board): "Which daily scripture reflection did you find most challenging or most interesting? Why?" In the groups, allow each person two minutes to respond.

Discussion of Blessed/Cursed Paraphrases

(If the group is large, you may subdivide to do steps 1–3 of this activity. If there are eight or fewer participants, the group as a whole can do the steps together.)

Step 1.   Invite group members to get out their journals/books to find their rewritten beatitude. Ask: "Did you find it difficult to rewrite this week's beatitude? Was it easier or harder this week than last?" Allow time for responses.

Step 2.   Ask, "Did writing an opposite to this beatitude lead you to any insights about it or about yourself?" Allow time for responses.

Step 3.   Invite all who wrote negative restatements of the beatitude to take turns reading them. After all have read, ask for general comments about the ideas.

Step 4.   Invite group members to read their positive restatements of the beatitude. After all have read, ask what ideas in the restatements members found helpful.

Step 5.   Ask the group to point out places where they hear consensus or similar ideas in the restatements of the beatitude. If time permits, construct a group restatement of "Blessed are the peacemakers . . ." from all the individual statements.

Moving Deeper

Step 1. Hand out copies of the ministry list. Say, "We're going to look at places in our world where shalom—peace, wholeness, security—is needed."

Step 2. Write the word *shalom* on the board/chart. Ask group members to suggest words that describe a world of shalom, where everyone's needs are met. List them on the board/chart.

Step 3. Holding up the newspaper, read headlines that relate to situations that reflect the opposite of the descriptions you listed for shalom. Ask: "What actions by people of faith could move these persons and situations closer to what we have described on this list? Do you know of things that are being done to address these situations mentioned in the newspaper?" Start another list of these suggestions/activities.

Step 4. Instruct the group to look at the list of your church's outreach ministries. Ask, "Which of these are moving the world toward peace and wholeness?" Invite any who have participated in these ministries to tell how these outreaches are doing that.

Step 5. Ask, "Can you think of other things we could do to work for peace in these situations?" Add these to the list begun in step 3.

Step 6. Ask, "Who would you name as a peacemaker who inspires you, and why?" Allow group members to name and describe these persons.

Commitment to Personal Response

Step 1. Start the meditative music. Tell participants that you are going to give them time to consider their response to this week's session.

Step 2. Read aloud this week's beatitude. Then ask, "Where do your gifts, your deep gladness, and the world's deep need for peace overlap?" Allow two minutes of silence for reflection.

Step 3. Ask, "Where is God calling you to be a peacemaker?" Allow a minute for reflection.

Step 4. Invite participants to note in their journal/book any insight or commitment they want to record.

Giving of Gifts

Give each person an adhesive bandage. Say, "Carry this in your wallet or purse as a reminder that you are called to play a part in Christ's work of bringing healing and wholeness in the world."

Closing Prayer

Invite group members to mention prayer concerns arising from the session and other concerns. Ask for a volunteer to pray, lead a closing prayer of your own creation, or pray this prayer:

> Creator and Healer of the world, help us to see our part in your work of healing our world and its wounded people. Show us what needs to be torn down and what needs to be built up, that all people may live in peace and safety, enjoying fullness of life. We especially ask your loving care for _____ *(name specific persons and needs mentioned by group members).* Amen.

Sending Forth

Say, "Go in peace as the children of God, for that is who you are."

SESSION 8: BLESSED ARE THOSE WHO ARE PERSECUTED

Supplies for This Session

☐ Christ candle/worship center materials
☐ Matches or candlelighter
☐ Chart-sized paper and markers or whiteboard and markers
☐ Hymnals and music leader (or recorded music and means to play it)
☐ Small crosses, one per participant

Preparing for This Session

Prepare a simple evaluation form with these questions, allowing space after each for answers: "What went well with this study? What could be improved? What did you learn?" If you prefer to do an oral evaluation, ask these questions at the end of the session and record responses. Pass on the evaluation results to the person responsible for adult education or small groups in your church and to Upper Room Books (1908 Grand Ave., Nashville, TN 37212) so we can use your comments to improve future resources.

Lighting the Christ Candle

Distribute the cards printed with the opening prayer if it will be prayed in unison. Invite the group members to quiet themselves. Light the Christ candle, saying, "We light this candle as a reminder that Christ is here with us and is a part of our conversations."

Opening Prayer

Say, "Join me in the opening prayer printed on the card," and begin praying; or, if your group is not using the same prayer each week, ask the person you invited ahead of time to pray or lead a prayer yourself.

Music/Singing

Sing "I Sing a Song of the Saints of God" (#712, *UMH*; #364, *PH*; #295, *NCH*; #293, *EH*) or "I Know Whom I Have Believed" (#714, *UMH*).

Reflection on Reading/Journaling/Personal Response Commitments

Step 1. Invite persons to comment within their groups on how it went with their personal response, whatever they committed to do. Remind them that no one is keeping score, that this is just a way of checking in. Allow each person one minute to respond.

Step 2. Ask participants to group themselves in threes. Remind them to give each person opportunity to respond to the questions before beginning any further discussion. Ask (or write on chart/board): "What passages in this week's reading caught your attention? How does the reading relate to your life?" Give each person two minutes to respond.

Step 3. Ask (or write on chart/board): "Which daily scripture reflection did you find most challenging or most interesting? Why?" In the groups, allow each person two minutes to respond.

Discussion of Blessed/Cursed Paraphrases

(If the group is large, you may subdivide to do steps 1–3 of this activity. If there are eight or fewer participants, the group as a whole can do the steps together.)

Step 1. Invite group members to get out their journals/books to find their rewritten beatitude. Ask, "Did you find it difficult to rewrite this week's beatitude? Was it easier or harder this week than last?" Allow time for responses.

Step 2. Ask, "Did writing an opposite to this beatitude lead you to any insights about it or about yourself?" Allow time for responses.

Step 3. Invite all who wrote negative restatements of the beatitude to read them, each person in turn. After all have read, ask for general comments about the ideas.

Step 4. Invite group members to read in turn their positive restatements of the beatitude. After all have read, ask what ideas in the restatements members found helpful.

Step 5. Ask the group to point out places where they hear consensus or similar ideas in the restatements of the beatitude. If time permits, construct a group restatement of "Blessed are those who are persecuted . . . " from all the individual statements.

Moving Deeper: Guest Speaker

Step 1. Introduce the speaker, or have the person who knows the speaker introduce him or her. After the speaker finishes, ask group members if they have questions. When the question-and-answer session ends, have someone escort the speaker out so the group can continue meeting.

Step 2. Ask, "What insights or responses do you have?" Allow time for discussion.

Commitment to Personal Response

Step 1. Start the meditative music. Tell participants that you are going to give them some time to consider their response to this week's session.

Step 2. Ask, "Have you ever experienced ridicule or persecution for being a Christian? If so, do you see it as a blessing? If not, do you see ways it could be a blessing?" Allow two minutes of silence for reflection.

Step 3. Ask, "What response is God asking of you? Do you feel an inner urging to make some response yourself? How can you support those who are persecuted for their faith in Christ?" Allow a minute of silence for reflection.

Step 4. Invite group members to note in their journal/book any insight or commitment they want to record.

Evaluation

Step 1. Hand out the evaluation forms you prepared, and allow five minutes for group members to complete them.

Step 2. Collect the completed forms.

Giving of Gifts

Give a cross to each group member and invite everyone to carry their cross as a reminder that following Christ does not mean taking the easy way.

Closing Prayer

Invite group members to mention prayer concerns arising from the session and other concerns. Ask for a volunteer to pray, lead a closing prayer of your own creation, or pray this prayer:

> O God, you know our hearts. You know how we shrink away from suffering. Give us courage to live for you every day, wherever we go, even if doing so brings persecution. We pray for all those who suffer for you. Grant them courage and unwavering faith. We pray also for those whose needs have been mentioned here, especially
> _____ (*name specific persons and needs mentioned by group members*). Be with them and let them feel your love surrounding them, as we feel your love surrounding and supporting us. Amen.

Sending Forth

Say, "Go in the power of Christ, who suffered for us and lives to bring us to eternal life."

Notes

CHAPTER 1

1. Rosemary Radford Ruether, *Women and Redemption: A Theological History* (Minneapolis, Minn.: Fortress Press, 1998), 17.
2. Ibid., 18.
3. Johannes Baptist Metz, *Poverty of Spirit,* trans. John Drury (Paramus, N.J.: Paulist Press, 1968), 47.

CHAPTER 6

1. Rick Warren, *The Purpose-Driven Life: What on Earth Am I Here For?* (Grand Rapids, Mich.: Zondervan, 2002), 235–36.
2. "Vocation," in *Wishful Thinking: A Theological ABC* by Frederick Buechner (New York: Harper & Row, Publishers, 1973), 95.
3. Tom Sine, "Crises Spur Christians to Connect Faith with Daily Life," *United Methodist Reporter,* January 4, 2002.

CHAPTER 7

1. John A. Sanford, *The Kingdom Within: A Study of the Inner Meaning of Jesus' Sayings* (New York: Paulist Press, 1970), 56.
2. Ibid., 57.
3. Ruether, *Women and Redemption,* 109.
4. Rubem Alves, *I Believe in the Resurrection of the Body,* trans. L.M. McCoy (Philadelphia, Pa.: Fortress Press, 1986), 70, 75.

CHAPTER 8

1. Martin Luther King Jr., "A Knock at Midnight," in *Strength to Love* (Philadelphia: Fortress Press, 1981), 57.
2. John A. Sanford, *The Kingdom Within,* 64–65.
3. From Søren Kierkegaard, "Followers, Not Admirers," cited on www.bruderhof.com.
4. Metz, *Poverty of Spirit,* 17.

For Further Reading

BOOKS ON PERSONAL MISSION AND SPIRITUAL GIFTS

Clapper, Gregory S. *Living Your Heart's Desire: God's Call and Your Vocation.* Nashville, Tenn.: Upper Room Books, 2005.

Covey, Stephen R. *The Eighth Habit: From Effectiveness to Greatness.* New York: Simon & Schuster, 2004.

Covey, Stephen R. *The 7 Habits of Highly Effective People: Powerful Lessons in Personal Change.* New York: Simon & Schuster, 1990.

Covey, Stephen R., A. Roger Merrill, and Rebecca R. Merrill. *First Things First.* New York: Simon & Schuster, 1994.

Sine, Tom, and Christine Sine. *Living on Purpose: Finding God's Best for Your Life.* Grand Rapids, Mich.: Baker Books, 2005.

Warren, Rick. *The Purpose-Driven Life: What on Earth Am I Here For?* Grand Rapids, Mich.: Zondervan, 2002.

CHAPTER 1: THE BLESSINGS OF POVERTY

Beasley-Topliffe, Keith, ed. *A Life of Total Prayer: Selected Writings of Catherine of Siena.* Nashville, Tenn.: Upper Room Books, 2000.

Birch, Bruce C., and Larry L. Rasmussen. *The Predicament of the Prosperous.* Louisville, Ky.: Westminster John Knox Press, 1981.

Law, William. *A Serious Call to A Devout and Holy Life.* Whitefish, Mont.: Kessinger, 2005.

Murray, Andrew. *Waiting on God: A Classic Devotional Edited for Today's Reader.* Grand Rapids, Mich.: Bethany House, 2001.

CHAPTER 2: THE GIFTS IN OUR GRIEVING

Beasley-Topliffe, Keith, ed. *Loving God through the Darkness: Selected Writings of John of the Cross.* Nashville, Tenn.: Upper Room Books, 2000.

Broyles, Anne C. *Journaling: A Spiritual Journey.* Nashville, Tenn.: Upper Room Books, 2002.

Clapper, Gregory S. *When the World Breaks Your Heart: Spiritual Ways of Living with Tragedy.* Nashville, Tenn.: Upper Room Books, 1999.

Gregg-Schroeder, Susan. *In the Shadow of God's Wings: Grace in the Midst of Depression.* Nashville, Tenn.: Upper Room Books, 1997.

Long, William, and Glandion C. Carney. *A Hard-Fought Hope: Journeying with Job through Mystery.* Nashville, Tenn.: Upper Room Books, 2005.

Nouwen, Henri J. M. *The Wounded Healer.* New York: Doubleday, 1999.

Redding, Mary Lou. *Breaking and Mending: Divorce and God's Grace.* Nashville, Tenn.: Upper Room Books, 1998.

Reeves, Nancy. *A Path through Loss: A Guide to Writing Your Healing and Growth.* Kelowna, British Columbia: Northstone, 2004.

CHAPTER 3: POWER UNDER GOD'S CONTROL

Beasley-Topliffe, Keith. *A Life of Total Prayer: Selected Writings of Catherine of Siena.* Nashville, Tenn.: Upper Room Books, 2000.

Brown, Patricia D. *Learning to Lead from Your Spiritual Center.* Nashville, Tenn.: Abingdon Press, 1996.

Miller, Wendy. *Jesus, Our Spiritual Director: A Pilgrimage through the Gospels.* Nashville, Tenn.: Upper Room Books, 2004.

CHAPTER 4: SATISFIED WITH BEING UNSATISFIED

Bender, Sheila. *Keeping a Journal You Love.* Cincinnati, Ohio: North Light Books, 2001.

Crain, Margaret Ann, and Jack Seymour. *Yearning for God: Reflections of Faithful Lives.* Nashville, Tenn.: Upper Room Books, 2003.

Dorff, Francis. *Simply SoulStirring: Writing as a Meditative Practice.* Mahwah, N.J.: Paulist Press, 1998.

James, William. *The Varieties of Religious Experience: A Study in Human Nature,* Centenary Edition. New York: Routledge, 2002.

Jenkins, J. Marshall. *A Wakeful Faith: Spiritual Practice in the Real World.* Nashville, Tenn.: Upper Room Books, 2000.

Kincannon, Karla. *Creativity and Divine Surprise: Finding the Place of Your Resurrection.* Nashville, Tenn.: Upper Room Books, 2005.

Mulholland, M. Robert, Jr. *Shaped by the Word: The Power of Scripture in Spiritual Formation.* Nashville, Tenn.: Upper Room Books, 2001.

Nouwen, Henri J. M. *Behold the Beauty of the Lord: Praying with Icons.* Notre Dame, Ind.: Ave Maria Press, 2004.

Wolpert, Daniel. *Creating a Life with God: The Call of Ancient Prayer Practices.* Nashville, Tenn.: Upper Room Books, 2004.

CHAPTER 6: TO WILL ONE THING

Clapper, Gregory S. *Living Your Heart's Desire: God's Call and Your Vocation.* Nashville, Tenn.: Upper Room Books, 2005.

Covey, Stephen R. *The 8th Habit: From Effectiveness to Greatness.* New York: Simon and Schuster, 2004.

Covey, Stephen R., A. Roger Merrill, and Rebecca R. Merrill. *First Things First.* New York: Simon and Schuster, 1996.

Myers, Isabel Briggs. *Gifts Differing: Understanding Personality Type.* Mountain View, Calif.: Consulting Psychologists Press, 1995.

Reeves, Nancy. *I'd Say Yes, God, If I Knew What You Wanted: Spiritual Discernment.* Kelowna, British Columbia: Northstone, 2001.

Vest, Norvene. *Friend of the Soul: A Benedictine Spirituality of Work.* Cambridge, Mass.: Cowley, 1997.

CHAPTER 7: SEEING THE WORLD NEEDY AND WHOLE

Fox, Matthew. *A Spirituality Named Compassion: Uniting Mystical Awareness with Social Justice.* Rochester, Vt.: Inner Traditions International, 1999.

Wallis, Jim. *God's Politics: Why the Right Gets It Wrong and the Left Doesn't Get It.* New York: HarperTrade, 2005.

CHAPTER 8: ACTION AND REACTION

Bonhoeffer, Dietrich. *Letters and Papers from Prison.* New York: Macmillan Publishing Company, 1981.

Companjen, Anneke. *Hidden Sorrow, Lasting Joy: The Forgotten Women of the Persecuted Church.* Wheaton, Ill.: Tyndale House Publishers, 2001.

Dunnam, Maxie. *Workbook on Lessons from the Saints.* Nashville, Tenn.: Upper Room Books, 2002.

Foxe, John. *Foxe's Book of Martyrs.* Uhrichsville, Ohio: Barbour, 2004.

Frank, Anne, et al. *The Diary of Anne Frank: The Critical Edition.* New York: Doubleday, 2003.

Hefley, James, and Marti Hefley. *By Their Blood: Christian Martyrs from the Twentieth Century and Beyond.* Grand Rapids, Mich.: Baker Book House, 2004.

Howell, James. *Servants, Misfits, and Martyrs: Saints and Their Stories.* Nashville, Tenn.: Upper Room Books, 2000.

Service Opportunities

Inviting Ministries

- [ ] Parking lot greeter—early service
- [ ] Parking lot greeter—late service
- [ ] Parking lot greeter—Special events
- [ ] Worship greeter—early service
- [ ] Worship greeter—late service
- [ ] Worship greeter—Saturday PM service
- [ ] Guest caller
- [ ] Shepherd Care leadership team
- [ ] Pew replenisher (prayer cards, visitor badges, etc.)
- [ ] Hospitality ministry team
- [ ] Attendance data entry
- [ ] Attendance data sorter
- [ ] Shepherd Care caller
- [ ] Guest data entry
- [ ] Help with Inviting Ministries Web site
- [ ] Special needs parking—early service
- [ ] Special needs parking—late service
- [ ] Special needs parking—special events
- [ ] Parking shuttle driver
- [ ] Parking hospitality team (provide coffee, badges, etc.)

Worship Ministries

- [ ] Communion service coordinator
- [ ] Communion server—early service
- [ ] Communion server—late service
- [ ] Communion server—Saturday PM service
- [ ] Usher—early service
- [ ] Usher—late service
- [ ] Usher—Saturday PM service
- [ ] Usher—Special events
- [ ] Scripture reader
- [ ] Altar Guild
- [ ] Worship videographer
- [ ] Sound technician

Music Ministries

- [ ] Adult choir
- [ ] Adult handbell choir
- [ ] Music office volunteer
- [ ] Pianist—children's choir
- [ ] Pianist—youth choir
- [ ] Pianist—adult choir
- [ ] Orchestral instrumentalist
- [ ] Praise band musician
- [ ] Youth choir auction—organizer
- [ ] Youth choir auction—setup
- [ ] Youth choir auction—fund-raiser
- [ ] Children's choir director
- [ ] Children's choir teacher
- [ ] Children's choir recreation
- [ ] Children's choir meal

Worship Arts

- [ ] Visual arts
- [ ] Liturgical movement
- [ ] Drama
- [ ] Banner group
- [ ] Costume design/seamstress
- [ ] Stage/set construction

Children's Ministries

- [ ] Nursery volunteer
- [ ] Children's church helper
- [ ] Coordinate one-time event
- [ ] Preschool Sunday school teacher
- [ ] Preschool outreach
- [ ] Elementary Sunday school teacher
- [ ] Children's outreach
- [ ] Saturday Bible study teacher
- [ ] Confirmation mentor
- [ ] Vacation Bible School volunteer
- [ ] Terrific Tuesday volunteer
- [ ] Photographer for children's events
- [ ] Children's council member
- [ ] Rosebud delivery to new parents

- ☐ Hall greeter Sunday morning
- ☐ Children's worship leadership team
- ☐ Wednesday night preschool helper

Youth Ministries

- ☐ Sunday school teacher
- ☐ Youth Bible study leader
- ☐ Junior high counselor
- ☐ Senior high counselor
- ☐ Event chaperone
- ☐ Help with mission project
- ☐ Provide food for youth events
- ☐ Sports coach
- ☐ Golf Scramble committee
- ☐ Golf Scramble volunteer
- ☐ Sunday youth prayer ministry
- ☐ Scout leader
- ☐ Media volunteer
- ☐ Office volunteer
- ☐ Praise band director

Adult Ministries

- ☐ Sunday school teacher
- ☐ Sunday school office helper
- ☐ Companions in Christ facilitator
- ☐ Women's circle leader
- ☐ Women's circle member
- ☐ Small-group leader
- ☐ Short-term study leader
- ☐ Library volunteer

Single Adult Ministry

- ☐ College/Young Adult ministry team
- ☐ Young adult service leadership team
- ☐ Singles council representative
- ☐ Singles Web site administrator
- ☐ Singles newsletter coordinator
- ☐ Program leader
- ☐ Social/fellowship long-range planning
- ☐ Dance lessons/events team
- ☐ Sports/hiking events team
- ☐ Spiritual and/or support programs
- ☐ Single Parent Action committee
- ☐ Outreach and service team

- ☐ Widow/widowers support team

Family & Leisure Ministries

- ☐ Help with fall picnic
- ☐ Help with Advent wreath making
- ☐ Coach boys'/girls' basketball
- ☐ Coach men's basketball
- ☐ Coach men's softball
- ☐ Coach youth volleyball

Healing Ministries

- ☐ Stephen Ministry
- ☐ Homebound ministry
- ☐ Blood donor
- ☐ Blood drive volunteer
- ☐ Intercessory prayer ministry
- ☐ Support groups team
- ☐ Disability awareness team

Equipping Ministries

- ☐ Ministry Discovery Workshop leader
- ☐ Recognition team
- ☐ Data entry team

Communications

- ☐ Web site maintenance team
- ☐ Monthly magazine development team
- ☐ Monthly magazine publication team
- ☐ Videographer for special events
- ☐ Photographer for special events
- ☐ Graphic designer for sermon series
- ☐ Graphic designer for seasonal emphasis

Building and Grounds

- ☐ Painting
- ☐ General maintenance
- ☐ Cleaning and general housekeeping
- ☐ Flower beds planting and maintenance
- ☐ Consultation
- ☐ After-hours front desk attendant

General Office Support

- ☐ Help with church mailings
- ☐ Worship bulletin stuffers
- ☐ Office volunteer
- ☐ Volunteer receptionist

Finance Department

- [ ] Help with church mailings
- [ ] Office volunteer/data entry
- [ ] Sunday worship service assistant

Community Outreach Opportunities

- [ ] Bethlehem Neighborhood Centers
- [ ] Better Decisions women's prison ministry
- [ ] Bridges of Williamson County (shelter/new-start programs)
- [ ] Campus for Human Development (homeless center)
- [ ] Community care fellowship
- [ ] Community outreach ministries
- [ ] Disaster relief—Local
- [ ] Weekday feeding program server
- [ ] Family Faith Clinic
- [ ] Friends Learning in Pairs (retired senior volunteers)
- [ ] Graceworks community thrift store
- [ ] Habitat for Humanity—food prep for workers
- [ ] Habitat for Humanity—fund-raising/materials donors
- [ ] Habitat for Humanity—worker recruitment
- [ ] Habitat for Humanity—on-site volunteer
- [ ] Habitat for Humanity—worker caller/reminder
- [ ] Health maintenance/preventive medicine
- [ ] Hobson UMC Partnership—tutor
- [ ] Hobson UMC Partnership—food program
- [ ] Hobson UMC Partnership—cooperative worship
- [ ] Hispanic Achievers program
- [ ] Humphrey's Street UMC
- [ ] Literacy Council of Williamson County
- [ ] The Manger Christmas store
- [ ] Miriam's Promise adoption ministry
- [ ] Nashville Rescue Mission feeding program server
- [ ] Room in the Inn homeless shelter
- [ ] Safe Haven Family Shelter—food prep
- [ ] Safe Haven Family Shelter—overnight host
- [ ] 61st UMC Partnership—food prep
- [ ] 61st UMC Partnership—tools
- [ ] 61st UMC Partnership—tutors (after-school program)
- [ ] YWCA Domestic Violence Center

Congregational Outreach Opportunities

- [ ] Adopt-a-Family
- [ ] Angel Tree Christmas gift program
- [ ] Christmas baskets
- [ ] Kids' Clothing Sale leadership team
- [ ] Kids' Clothing Sale set-up/take-down
- [ ] Kids' Clothing Sale check-in/check-out
- [ ] Kids' Clothing Sale register clerk
- [ ] Kids' Clothing Sale general volunteer
- [ ] Prison ministry Bible study
- [ ] Sower's Fund for Emergency Assistance

National Mission Opportunities

- [ ] Disaster Relief—National

International Mission Opportunities

- [ ] Healing Wings
- [ ] Honduras Medical Mission
- [ ] Mexico mission partnership
- [ ] Russia mission partnership
- [ ] South Africa mission partnership

*This list is adapted from Brentwood United Methodist Church's service commitment card. Used by permission of Brentwood United Methodist Church, 309 Franklin Road, Brentwood, TN 37027.

WHERE IS GOD CALLING YOU TO SERVE?

The following are opportunities for ministry in relation to seventeen spiritual gifts. With your shape for ministry in mind (spiritual gifts, passion, abilities, personality style, and experiences), explore the ministries you may be called to.

Administration

Altar Guild
Arts & crafts
Building & grounds
Church council
Clerical/office help
Event coordinator
Fall picnic
Finances
Food service
Fund-raising
Library volunteer
Long-range planning
Mailings
Ministry fair
Music library
Newsletter
Parking lot greeter
Prepare church packets
Printing
Publicity
Radio/TV ministry
Robe attendant
Snack supper coordinator
Sunday school office helper
Supply room coordinator
Task force leader
Tax consultant
Web site entry/design

Apostleship

Advocacy volunteer
College/Young Adult ministry
Confirmation mentor
ESL tutor
Evangelism
Habitat for Humanity
Homeless ministry
Literacy tutor
Media

Men's ministry
Mentoring
Mission trip
Multicultural ministry
Social justice issues
Visitation
Women's ministry

Discernment

Bible study leader
Counseling
Chaperone
College/Young Adult ministry
Companions in Christ facilitator
Confirmation Friend in Faith
Confirmation mentor
Crisis phone counselor
Grief support volunteer
Lead short-term study
Lead Wednesday night class
Leadership team
Ministry team/council
Pray for children
Prayer ministry
Small-group leader
Social action ministries
Spiritual retreat planning
Staff-Parish Relations Committee
Support group facilitator
Teacher
Trustee

Exhortation

First-time guest caller
Accompanist
Banner making
Bible study leader
Big Brothers/Sisters
Care callers
Coaching

Choir
Clowning
College/Young Adult ministry
Communication
Communion server
Companions in Christ facilitator
Confirmation Friend in Faith
Confirmation mentor
Counseling
Drama
Group facilitator
Handbells
Homebound visitation
Instrumentalist
Lead short-term study
Lead Wednesday night class
Leadership Team
Liturgical dance
Media
Ministry fair
Ministry Discovery Workshop leader
Ministry liaison
Ministry team/council
Miriam's Promise
Newcomers ministry
Nursing home visitation
Praise band
Pray for children
Prayer ministry
Radio/TV ministry
Scripture reader
Signing
Small-group leader
Teacher
Web site entry/design
Worship greeter

Evangelism

First-time guest caller

Big Brothers/Sisters
Care caller
Care card sender
Choir
Clowning
Communication
Community outreach
ministry
Concerts
Confirmation Friend in Faith
Confirmation mentor
Discipleship
Drama
Greeters
Guest data entry
Handbells
Homeless ministry
Instrumentalist
Liturgical dance
Media
Missions
Newcomer ministry
Photographer
Praise band
Radio/TV ministry
Shepherd Care Team
Signing
Storyteller
Usher
Videographer
Visitation
Web site entry/design
Wednesday night host/
hostess
Worship greeter

Faith
Assist special-needs children
Bible study leader
Companions in Christ
facilitator
Confirmation Friend in Faith
Confirmation mentor
Counseling
Drama
Healing Team
Missions
Nursery

Prayer ministry
Teaching

Giving
AIDS Angel Tree
Benevolence
Blood donor
Christmas baskets
Community Outreach
ministry
Stewardship Emphasis Team

Healing
Blood donor
Counseling
Community outreach
ministry
Elder care
Grief support
Healing worship service
Homebound visitation
Hospice volunteer
Hospital volunteer
Marriage mentoring
Nurse/physician
Nursing home visitor
Pray for children
Prayer ministry
Senior adult ministry
Transportation/errand
volunteer
Volunteer receptionist—
counseling center

Helps
Arts & crafts
Advent wreath making
Altar Guild
Building & grounds
Carpentry
Cleaning
Clerical
Construction
Data entry
Decorating
Electrical
Facility maintenance
Fall picnic
Floral arrangements
Food services

Guest data entry
Habitat for Humanity house
Handyman ministry
Parking lot greeter
Prepare church packets
Radio/TV ministry
Snack supper coordinator
Snack supper volunteer
Transportation
Van driver
Worship greeter

Knowledge
Bible study leader
Church council
Companions in Christ facili-
tator
College/Young Adult ministry
Confirmation Friend in Faith
Confirmation mentor
Finance Committee
Lay Ministry Team
Lead short-term study
Lead Wednesday night class
Leadership Team
Ministry Discovery Workshop
leader
Personnel
Publicity
Small-group leader
Staff-Parish Relations Com-
mittee
Stewardship Emphasis Team
Teacher
Trustee
Tutoring
Writing
Youth ministry

Leadership
Church council
Coaching
Confirmation mentor
Lay Ministry Team
Long-range planning
Ministry Discovery Workshop
leader
Personnel
Small-group leader

Song leader
Spiritual retreat planning
Staff-Parish Relations Committee
Teaching
Women's mission group
Youth ministry

Mercy

Adult literacy
AIDS Angel Tree
Assist special-needs children
Big Brothers/Sisters
Christmas baskets
Counseling
Disaster relief
Elder care
EMT
Grief support
Habitat House
Handyman ministries
Homebound visitation
Homeless ministry
Hospital volunteer
Hospice volunteer
Men's mission group
Mission trip
Prayer ministry
Women's mission group

Prophecy

Bible study leader
Children's ministry
Church council
College/Young Adult ministry
Communication
Companions in Christ facilitator
Confirmation mentor
Leadership Team
Long-range planning
Ministry Team/Council
Prayer ministry
Small-group leader
Teaching
Youth ministry

Pastor/Shepherd

Bible study leader

Care caller
Communion server
Companions in Christ facilitator
Confirmation Friend in Faith
Confirmation mentor
Counseling
Elder care
Grief support volunteer
Help with healing service
Lay Ministry Team
Pray for children
Prayer ministry
Robe attendant
Small-group leader
Support group facilitator
Transportation/errand volunteer
Wednesday night host/hostess
Youth ministry
Visitation

Service

First-time guest caller
Accompanist
Altar Guild
Banner making
Care caller
Care card sender
Chaperone
Child care
Children's ministries
Choir
Communication
Communion server
EMT
Handbells
Hospital volunteer
Instrumentalist
Liturgical dance
Men's missions
Ministry fair
Mission trip
Nursery volunteer
Office volunteer
Parking lot greeter
Pew replenisher

Pizza/movie night
Praise band
Serving meals
Single Parent Network volunteer
Singles Sunday Fellowship volunteer
Song leader
Sound technician
Special Olympics
Usher
Weddings
Women's missions

Teaching

Adult literacy tutor
Arts & Crafts
Bible study leader
Chaperone
Children's ministry
Coaching
Communication
Group facilitator
Leadership training
Library volunteer
Ministry Discovery Workshop leader
Ministry Team/Council
School aide
Song leader
Sunday school teacher
Tutoring
Vacation Bible School
Youth ministry

Wisdom

Companions in Christ facilitator
Counseling
Crisis phone counselor
Intercessory prayer
Lay Ministry Team
Ministry Team/Council
Small-group leader
Staff-Parish Relations Committee
Support group facilitator
Writing

About the Author

Mary Lou Redding serves as managing editor of *The Upper Room* daily devotional guide. In addition, she leads retreats and writers' workshops in the U.S. and abroad. Her writings have appeared in numerous magazines, including *Alive Now, Weavings, Christian Writer,* and *Solo.* She is the author of *While We Wait: Living the Questions of Advent* (Upper Room Books, 2002) and *Breaking and Mending: Divorce and God's Grace* (Upper Room Books, 1998) and contributed to the *Spiritual Formation Bible* (Zondervan, 1999).

Mary Lou received her Bachelor of Arts degree in English Literature from Oral Roberts University and her Master of Arts in Rhetoric and Writing from the University of Tulsa. She has pursued further study at Vanderbilt University and completed the two-year Academy of Spiritual Formation offered by The Upper Room.

Mary Lou has one adult daughter and one granddaughter, Rosalie. She loves word games and racquetball and is an Atlanta Braves fan.